Books by Paul J. Bucknell

Allowing the Bible to speak to our lives today!

- ✦ *Overcoming Anxiety: Finding Peace, Discovering God*
- ✦ *Reaching Beyond Mediocrity: Faith's Triumph Over Temptation*
- ✦ *The Life Core: Discovering the Heart of Great Training*
- ✦ *Life in the Spirit! Experiencing the Fullness of Christ*
- ✦ *The Godly Man: When God Touches a Man's Life*
- ✦ *Redemption Through the Scriptures/ Study Guide*
- ✦ *Godly Beginnings for the Family*
- ✦ *Principles and Practices of Biblical Parenting*
- ✦ *Building a Great Marriage*
- ✦ *The Lord Your Healer: Discover Him and Find...*
- ✦ *Christian Premarital Counseling Manual for Counselors*
- ✦ *Relational Discipleship: Cross Training*
- ✦ *A Spiritual Map for Unity*
- ✦ *Running the Race: Overcoming Lusts*
- ✦ *The Bible Teaching Commentary on Genesis*
- ✦ *The Bible Teaching Commentary on Romans*
- ✦ *Book of Romans: Bible Study Questions*
- ✦ *Book of Ephesians: Bible Studies*
- ✦ *Walking with Jesus: Abiding in Christ*
- ✦ *Inductive Bible Studies in Titus*
- ✦ *Life Transformation: A Monthly ... on Romans 12:9-21*
- ✦ *1 Peter Bible Study Questions: Living in a Fallen World*
- ✦ *Satan's Four Stations: The Destroyer is Destroyed*
- ✦ *3 X E Discipleship (Discipler and Disciple)*
- ✦ *Take Your Next Step into Ministry*
- ✦ *Training Leaders for Ministry*
- ✦ *Study Guide for Jonah: Understanding God's Heart*
- ✦ Check out our Discipleship Digital Libraries at
  www.foundationsforfreedom.net || www.bffbible.org

The Life Core

Discovering the Heart of Great Training

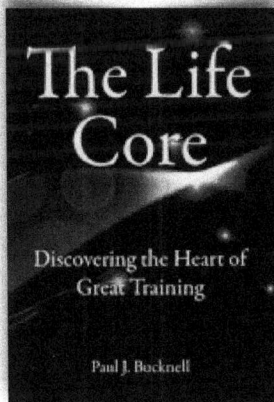

Paul J. Bucknell

Book Information

The Life Core: Discovering the Heart of Great Training

Copyright © 2012, Updated 2014, 2019 by Paul J. Bucknell
ISBN: 978-1-61993-026-1

E-Book:
ISBN: 978-1-61993-007-0

Also available in Burmese, Chinese, Cebuano, Hindi, Spanish, and Swahili

www.foundationsforfreedom.net
Pittsburgh, PA 15212 USA

The NASB version is used unless otherwise stated.
New American Standard Bible ©1960, 1995 used by permission, Lockman Foundation www.lockman.org.

Table of Contents

(1) Discover the Life Core
Chapters 1-8

(2) Appreciate the Life Core
Chapters 9-18

(3) Practice the Life Core
Chapters 19-29

(4) Implement the Life Core
Chapters 33-40

~ Appendices ~
#1-6

Tribute

Every gardener plants his garden in hope of a bountiful crop. God, the True Gardener, has planted His seed of life, watered it with His Spirit and will see it grow up into a great field of righteousness spread across the world!

For as the earth brings forth its sprouts, and as a garden causes the things sown in it to spring up, so the Lord God will cause righteousness and praise to spring up before all the nations (Isaiah 61:11).

We are completely and thankfully indebted to Him who has given us life and empowered us to do His gracious will.

Special Appreciation

Special thanks to Kurt Jorgensen in his friendship and careful help editing this book! A special thanks also to Kin Wee Choo who labored with me in better organizing this book as he labored over the Chinese translation.

Preface

The challenge is staggering—make disciples of all nations. The church has spread across the globe, but desperately few churches know what discipleship is or how to make disciples. The church suffers as a result. Discipleship remains largely out of the field of vision because the concept has not yet engaged our hearts.

The situation is quickly worsening due to the relentless barrage of images and sounds we endure daily due to the overstimulation of the media. Unbelief follows dissatisfaction. Instead of telling others what God has done for them, believers are wondering why God hasn't done more in their lives.

Think of a balloon. Without air, it is shapeless, lacks movement and ability to provide fun. Similarly, a kite without a frame lays on the ground even if the wind is blowing. A frame is needed to make the kite soar high in the sky.

Without Christ and His amazing work in our lives, our bodies are like flowers that blossom one day and fade the next. It is only the powerful Word of God through His Spirit that swirls into our beings producing new life and giving spiritual shape, power, and purpose (1 Peter 1:24-25). Oh, that we could remember that without Christ, we are nothing, but with Him, He can and will magnify His marvelous grace by working in and through our lives.

The Life Core identifies the underlying cause of this crisis in the Christian church and proposes practical solutions by showing how to bring God's life into our hearts and into the church through proper leadership training.

Besides the appendices which hold four insightful summary charts, there are four major sections taking us through the process of observing, welcoming, practicing, and incorporating life's truths into our lives and ministries. This not-so-secret work of God, like gravity, though always present, awaits our discovery and purposed commitment to make the most of it. Renewal depends on this rediscovery.

The first of four sections makes us aware of God's marvelous work in us. That discovery, however, must be followed (section two) by observing and welcoming His Spirit's work in our lives. As the sun's core with its fusion power, God dynamically works towards bringing each of His children to full maturity in Christ. Renewal comes as we strip away those things that hide this incredible work of Christ from each believer. As individuals and churches, we gain inner power as we contemplate this marvelous work of God within us. We are not fascinated with ourselves and accomplishments but with how God graciously works within us.

Section three carefully traces, stage by stage, how to practically accompany the Spirit of God as He trains us and others. Key insights on discipleship and mentoring help us practically implement these tools of training. The last main section suggests how to carry out The Life Core principles in specific contexts like churches, seminaries, and Christian schools. God's leaders need to apply the power of God's Word into their lives to lead and equip others to life transformation.

Study points, verses to meditate on, and application questions accompany each chapter. The survival of the church and its many resource arms like schools, churches, and seminaries can only find hope in this rediscovery of the Life Core truths.

The Life Core has an audio/video teaching companion. *Fostering Spiritual Growth in the Church* that shares about the heart of discipleship and how to practically foster growth at different stages of spiritual life, for yourself and others! This is found in the *BFF Discipleship #1 Digital Library* along with audio/video resources for *The Life Core*.[1]

---

[1] www.foundationsforfreedom.net/Help/Store/Intros/DLibrary-D1.html

Let the truth of God's Word flourish, and the people of God be revived! Completion of our mission as the church can be accomplished, but it requires a clearer understanding of how Christians grow in their faith. God's purpose is twofold: Deeply experience the Lord's presence through the Gospel and pass this same knowledge, joy, and passion onto others. May the Spirit's fire glow more brightly in each of our hearts as we seek to glorify God's work in our midst!

2012, updated 2014, 2019

Rev. Paul J. Bucknell

(1) Discover the Life Core

Chapters 1-8

The Life Core

#1 A Success Story

A dark cloud of failure has settled over the Christian church. It is bad enough to have an oppressive culture aggressively suppressing the Christian's freedom to express his life and worship, but the commitment to moral living is eroding away. Pastors and believers alike are divorcing, being stained with pornography, gambling, and flirting with the world.

Even worse, the foundation of the family is cracking. Our children's love for the Lord is waning. Something is obviously drastically wrong in the church when statistics show a large majority of our teens that have grown up in our churches are leaving the Lord and the church.

Dangers lurk all about us. I doubt more is needed to be stated since the decay in the church is so evident.

A spirit of defeat is creeping across the land. When it comes upon us, we feel like giving up. At times, we even question whether the truths we have devoted ourselves to are actually true and best.

What can be done?

One of the best ways to combat this evil temptation of defeat is to return to scriptural basics. "What then shall we say to these things? If God is for us, who is against us?" (Romans 8:31). God really is for us.

The Old Testament has many success stories. They are not like the typical success story that displays the cleverness of man. They instead paint a picture of man at his darkest time facing horrible defeat. Only at that point does the Bible show how God intervenes and marvelously rescues those who call upon His Name.

These true stories remind us of unchanging truths. We likewise, even at this evil time, can rely on God's extraordinary strength and see His delivery. We might not know what God is doing overall, but we do know how He wants to work in our lives at this present time. The Lord wants to strengthen us to complete the work He has committed to us.

The more we remember the power of the life within, the more we will sense God's strength within. We will not need to hunt after resources out there to cope. He wants to be the One we trust in. The Word of God reminds us that He is on our side. It would be a genuine boost to our spiritual life if we knew and believed that this is all that is really needed. God has made us to succeed, "and having done everything, to stand firm" (Ephesians 6:13). God's people can stand firm because God is not in the least worried about the enemy. Neither do we need to worry.

Our greatest danger

God, like a strong river, constantly draws us downstream into greater growth. Our greatest danger is to allow our raft to float to the river's edge and get out. Christians must stand attentive and engaged. We fight by constantly making ourselves aware of the truths of God so that he can safely guide us through life's

turmoil even when temptations come to our backdoor with their devilish suggestions.

There is no power or force greater than God that can frustrate His good purposes. If we are with Him–or more rightly stated–if He is with us, then we can accomplish all that the Lord wants to do through our lives. We can make those decisions to trust Him even in the worst conflicts by affirming what He says is true and then trusting Him.

As we increasingly become aware of God's constant, powerful and relevant activity in our lives, we will grow in our trust in Him and will find how His amazing peace keeps our hearts during tumultuous times. This awareness and assurance of God's presence becomes a powerful force in our lives.

Lessons

- The war is won. God won. We need to constantly remember God's power and put our trust in Him.
- The Lord desires to empower us–like Joseph, Daniel, Jesus–so that we can, like them, keep close to God so that He can accomplish His will through our lives.

Memorize & Meditate

Romans 8:31

Ephesians 6:13

Assignment

➡ Are you spiritually wounded? In what areas do you sense defeat? List the ones that come first to your mind.

-
-

- •

- •

➡ If you have stepped out of your raft of Christian faith, tell the Lord you are sorry by confessing your doubts, claiming forgiveness, getting back in, and continuing on down the river.

➡ Pray aloud right now (or write it down) that no matter what it takes, you are going to stay in the fight–even when the fighting gets tough. Praise Him for being the victor and His willingness to accompany us even in the most desperate circumstances to bring glory to His Name.

#2 Perspective Counts

Perspective shapes the way we think, approach life's difficulties, and try to solve problems.

Our perspective can help or hurt us, depending on how biblical they are. For example, the world looks very different from space than it does from earth. It is the same world but a different vantage point.

Biblical perspectives

Biblical perspectives provide an accurate grid through which to view the world. The more our concepts embrace untruthful assumptions, they hinder our spiritual development to be more like Christ and to carry out His good works.

It should be obvious to the church that it has clutched to false perspectives when it no longer lives out a godly, vivacious faith. A weak church and ungodly behaviors reveal our failing faith in Christ. At the same time it demonstrates that we possess a greater faith and trust in something else (i.e., idols).

The world is invading the heart and home through modern technology. This generation is, in many cases, unknowingly being persuaded by godless resources in all its forms, whether music, video, literature, etc. The world's immorality threatens our welfare because we unknowingly adopting the world's mindset. We can no longer keep our Christian home or church protected from evil if we invite it in.

Making important choices

The church is much like a nation during a civil war. We are forced to train our children, though we detest it, to take sides and fight. We, the church, will either train our children to be spiritually strong, or they will succumb to the surrounding forces, much like Israel had to resist the surrounding nations.

The Christian church around the globe suffers the same problem. This revolution is invading every country and culture with online connectivity. I just returned from training pastors and Christian leaders in a small city in southern Malawi. Guess what I discovered? The youth were surfing the web with smart phones. They are so poor, yet the world's influence is leaping over borders and poverty to shape their minds.

The invasion has come. The need to sharpen our biblical knowledge and commitment is urgent as the world with all its boasting, arrogance and false thinking encroaches on our minds.

Even if we awaken the church to the danger, does this solve the problem? No. Entrenched perspectives die hard. It is hard to admit the folly of our mistakes, but all along, the Lord has been providing what we needed to fight and win. Believers however, like a man who holds a sword for the first time, have been completely ineffective in proving His Word.

Change is coming

Change must come. It will come, but hopefully not by further enslavement to the ways of the world. We must discern God's truths and ride to victory by training others in righteousness.

Please do not be mistaken—we are not talking about new truths, but the trusted Word of God. "Every word of God is tested; He is a shield to those who take refuge in Him" (Proverbs 30:5). Nothing has changed.

Our vulnerabilities are being revealed. Darkness is encroaching upon the church. Now is the time to return to a biblical mindset. Our perspective of Christian education has become, for the most part, too influenced by the world's methods. Those graduating from seminaries and Christian schools are not being rightly trained, and it shows in their compromised living and their ineffectual ministry in the churches.

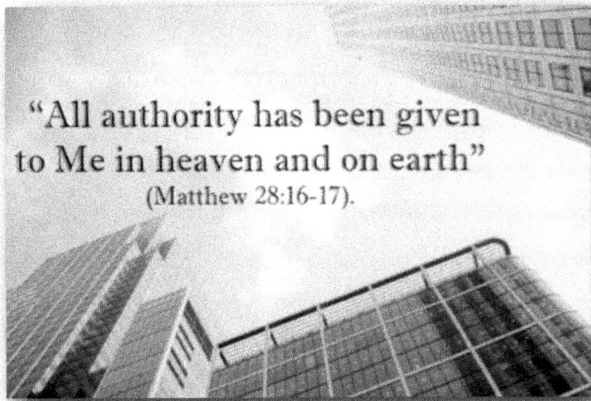

"All authority has been given to Me in heaven and on earth" (Matthew 28:16-17).

God's perspectives

We need God's perspective on our circumstances. What do we see? God has given the church all she needs to grow strong and vibrant, whether in the West or East. He has made it so that His people can reflect Christ's likeness in character, faith, and zeal to accomplish our Father's work.

"And when they saw Him, they worshiped Him; but some were doubtful. And Jesus came up and spoke to them, saying, 'All authority has been given to Me in heaven and on earth'" (Matthew 28:16-17). God has promised to give us all that we need just as He gave the Israelites authority to conquer the Promised Land. Jesus Christ has the authority. Do we believe or doubt the Word of God?

Lessons

- The church around the world is in a perilous state due to the world's increasing influence on our minds and lives.
- The church stands in a land of opportunity to break out of its old skins and adopt the full glory of God's truth for themselves and those around the world.

Memorize & Meditate

Proverbs 30:5

Matthew 28:16-17

Assignment

➡ Do you think the church, having the truth of God along with His promises and presence, can overcome that which threatens the church? Or do you, like the disciples of old, have some doubt? If so, what do you doubt?

➡ Think specifically about your circumstances; mark the places you see victory as well as defeat.

- Personal lives

- Work

- Family & home

- Ministry

- Other

#3 Change Must Come

Our choice

Our life

Changes make us uncomfortable so we tend to resist them. One Bible professor complained to me that his school is forcing all the professors to use computers! Such change is minor, however, compared to the genuine challenges facing the church; its very survival hangs in the balance.

The crisis looms

Grow or die. Be victorious or suffer defeat. These are our choices. All around us churches are waning. At on time it used to be that liberal churches were dying off, but now it's even the evangelical churches. How can this be? The outside world wrongly assumes that the message is irrelevant and impotent, but can we blame them? Once the church lays aside its faith in Jesus, it becomes irrelevant. Its power is lost.

The information network has sped up the assault by throwing gigabytes of data at us, dazzling our eyes and minds. Has God has opened up this flood of knowledge to accelerate the distribution of His truth? Of course, at the same time the enemy is using these same tools for his diabolical plans.

We should not feel overwhelmed, however. God is there to help us battle the enemy no matter what arms the evil one chooses to fight with. Although Satan's means of tackling God's people might change, his tactics remain the same. God's ability to help His people stands firm.

God's hidden participation

Even though the early church was scattered about, running in every direction, much likes ants dealing with a squashed anthill, God was still with each of them, never leaving their side. "So then those who were scattered because of the persecution that occurred in connection with Stephen..." (Acts 11:19).

Was God watching over the church? Certainly He was. He used this period of oppression to more quickly spread His Word through the church and thus disseminate His truth. The persecution served His greater purposes.

What do we find in Acts 13? A church, partly comprised of those scattered disciples, which was shaped and ready for God's mission to the world. "Now there were at Antioch, in the church... While they were ministering..." (Acts 13:1-3).

Some of God's people are facing subtle or outright persecution like in Acts 13. One of my pastor friends in a South Asian country gets regular hints, couched in threats to his life, to stop distributing tracts.

Others, though, are facing threats of irrelevance. The church continues the same activities as before, but they do not carry the same influence. Even little league baseball games keep God's people away from worship!

Looking for solutions

There is a tendency to make our worship services shorter. We say it is for the seekers, but deep down God's people like it too. We get to go home earlier and do what we want. Few are the ones that spend even ten minutes of their many hours of free time to pray. The excitement of God's Word is gone because we no longer see how it helps us in our lives.

Nothing has really changed, however. God's Word can powerfully speak to any generation in any culture or religion in the world, including the post-modern mind. Our old methods of feeding and maintaining the churches are inadequate for the invasion of worldly thought that has come on the people of God.

The question is, "How are we going to change things?" A new program? Advanced studies? All of this is too late and too slow. Already God's people around the world are suffering from the lack of the power of truth shining in their compromised lives.

Just take a look at the average marriage. Do we see God's love, care and harmony there? I train pastors around the world and even hold marriage training for them. Shepherds and sheep, share the same horrible marriages and serious problems.[2]

Identify the underly problem

I have seen God's Spirit mightily save great groups of people in various cultures, but the following generations are more objective and reject the hatred and anger problems that are not properly eliminated by the love of God working in their parents. They end up despising what they have been taught. This is the generational rejection that is alive wherever Christ's truth has gone but not fully adopted (Judges 1:2-3).

Though hardly against miracles and healing, seeking to have another wave of them will not bring us to where we need to be. I have witnessed how many strong leaders were wonderfully saved or helped by God through some special means, but this does not, in many cases, help them properly relate to their wives. We need to go beyond finding help for one area of our lives to being

---

[2] https://vimeo.com/channels/170337/19698044

a strong and pure people of God, that is, people in which each area of our lives are touched by the holy presence of God.

These problems have been perpetuated by the training taking place in churches and Christian schools. They have lacked an overall methodology to connect people to the simple, powerful gospel of Christ.

Unbelief is our underlying problem. Our personal experiences tend to shape our perspectives. Due to our failure to live out a fulfilling Christian life, we lose confidence and hope in God's Word. Unbelief grows. Toleration of lower standards and declining expectations ride piggyback on the shoulders of this unbelief.

Change is needed

We must change or be further absorbed into the world. New programs offer some change, but they are superficial, neglecting to deal with the fundamental problems. The same problems continue on.

We applaud those pastors, teachers, and evangelists who work harder. They think if they only speak louder or generate more emotion of love, God's people will be helped. This does not work.

Others entertain alternatives such as switching churches, denominations, or will even try out Eastern religions, TM, yoga, etc. They are hoping that these things will offer what they are looking for. They don't because these things lead away from the source of life, Jesus the Christ.

The path back home

We must return to Him. Repentance is our pathway back to God. "Repent therefore and return, that your sins may be wiped away, in order that times of refreshing may come from the presence of the Lord" (Acts 3:19). But let's not make this another methodology—stirring people to make a gesture of change rather than provoking the needed inward change.

Awakenings are due to genuine repentance taking place in many hearts at the same time and place. It is these individual changes that are really needed to change the overall direction of our culture. Don't think of a tame wave at the ocean held back by a slight grade at the shoreline, but a tsunami that breaks through our traditional approach of marking time in our 'Christian' lives.

Though the amount of sacrifices offered was impressive, the rededication of the temple only became an extraordinary celebration largely due to Solomon's prayer on the behalf of God's people. We need a heart that leads us back to the altar where we pray like Solomon, "If my people...humble themselves and pray, and seek My face and turn from their wicked ways, then I will hear from heaven, will forgive their sin, and will heal their land" (2 Chronicles 7:13-14).

There is no other way. We must always return to the altar where forgiveness can be found. No matter how bad things were, whether blight, famine, or even captivity, if Israel would turn toward the altar, God would hear and heal. Under the new covenant, our altar is Jesus Christ who can forgive and desires to restore us.

Returning to the Lord

The problems the church faces in this generation are not small. We are not trying to minimize them with Bible verses. Instead, we are using the little faith we have to begin opening our hearts to bring us to where we can again grasp God's perspective on what needs to be done.

God has no fear of this explosion of knowledge. He is utilizing it! His plan is not wavering under Satan's attack. The Lord sits in heaven and laughs at His enemies (Psalm 2). We need to prepare our hearts for what God wants by humbling our hearts, coming to the Lord on our knees and confessing our unbelief–we just don't believe the gospel is relevant and powerful enough for today.

If we come to Him, then He will come and show us how the church can powerfully confront the darkness in the world with His light.

Lessons

- God uses the attacks upon the church to press us into a corner so that we will break out of our old perspectives and again discover the power of His glorious truths.

- The real problem that the church faces is unbelief.

- Change begins by returning to God, humbling our hearts and confessing our sins.

- God's people must act or lose ground against our enemies.

Memorize & Meditate

2 Chronicles 7:14

2 Chronicles 6-7

Nehemiah 1 (View video). www.foundationsforfreedom.net/References/ OT/Historical/Nehemiah/Nehemiah01_Prayers_Video.html

Assignment

➡ Are you broken by sin in and around you, or do you just accept it as the way things happen to be?

➡ Like Nehemiah, come to God's altar not just for your sins of a straying heart and eye, but also for how God's people have needlessly wallowed about in defeat and despair rather than living in the full power of the Lord.

#4 Life's Glorious Expression

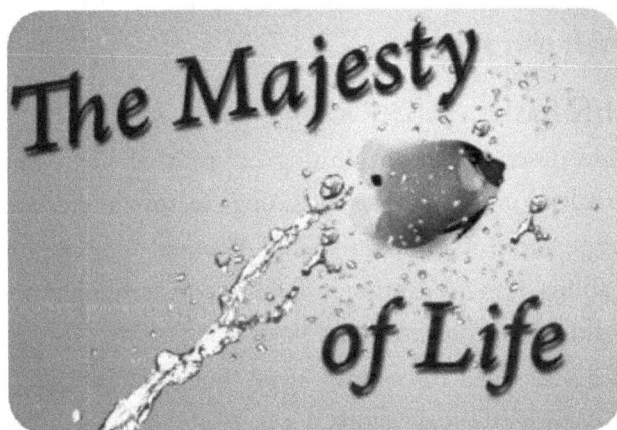

Life is a marvelous mystery that holds the world's greatest secrets. We all know what physical life is, but we only can define it by observation: it moves, breathes, reproduces, grows, eats, etc. Although we applaud humanity's accomplishment in mapping our DNA, we still are in the dark when it comes to explaining the nature of life.

Spiritual life is a topic that Christians often talk about, but the reality is that we are stifled by ignorance. Fortunately, we have the scriptural clues we need to unlock its potential effect on our lives.

Analogies of life

Scriptural authors and John in particular were amazed by symbols such as light, love and life. The important spiritual truths that God wanted to communicate to us have analogies in the physical creation of this world.

Of these three, life is the most fundamental. John said, "In Him was life, and the life was the light of men" (John 1:4). John was speaking, of course, about Jesus. Jesus had life and this life brought understanding and clarity to mankind.

This basic notion of life is critical to gaining a good understanding of discipleship. The more we grasp the concept of life, the easier we can clutch the meaning of other truths. Life is the frame on which all the other truths hang. (See appendix 2 for further reference.)

New life basics

New life describes the beginning of spiritual life. When we sought salvation, many of us, including me, sought eternal life as an escape from God's judgment. We had no clue to the implications of that salvation. Of course, if we thought about it, we would know that life must have a beginning. This is often taught by the need to be born again, but rarely, are we taught how this spiritual life develops.

Life is a frame on which all the other truths can hang.

Theology classes include teaching on holiness and sanctification (very important topics no doubt), but they are presented more in terms of concepts rather than the practical steps to spiritual living. So much so, that although many can describe what sanctification is, few can explain how spiritual life can be gained.

Our own ignorance and inability to grow in our relationship with God is only one side of the problem. These things are also being ignored or being improperly taught. What we do not know, we can't teach others.

Hidden from sight

Church leaders have been content to wrap up these treasures of truth in such a way that only seminarians and theologians can understand. This is contrary to how Jesus Christ used our daily experiences to communicate life's important truths to us.

These vital truths, then, become unlearnable except to those who love theology books. This is interesting because it seems that theologians often become the most cold and hostile to these teachings. Maybe they are being kept hidden from their sight?

In any case, God's people sitting on their pews or mats, depending where they worship, love getting to know God. However, they remain largely ignorant of how to practically grow in their special relationship with God. Some are oblivious even to the personal relationship they have with God. Precious truths are locked up and out of reach.

Finding life

Fortunately, there have been a few movements that have focused on spiritual growth, such as the Keswick Movement, but these are very limited. We might also think of the powerful revivals that have radically reshaped God's people when He opened their hearts and minds to His truths. I wonder, though, whether there was an overemphasis on experience compared to instruction. They did not need to learn how to come into God's presence as He revealed Himself in His radiant glory. They easily sensed His presence.

There has been much discussion of gifts and healings. They are important to the church of God and for some are 'recovered' truths, but they are hardly the central focus of the church, at least they should not be. Though spiritual growth does come through the growth of faith from miracles, this is for a minority number of God's people to establish a basic faith leading to spiritual growth, but they are not the typical means God uses for most of His people. They are meant to confirm Christ's work in us, not to become our all in all.

God has greater goals for miracles. They are only a beginning. For example, though one can be healed of a back injury and find Christ, he still needs to learn to control his anger by the power of the Holy Spirit. The healing opened his heart, but that is not the same as the ability to control his tongue when he is angry (Ephesians 4:16-29). If he does not learn how the Spirit can help him with this, then he will berate his wife and possibly carry on with a domineering spirit at church.

Spiritual disciplines

Christian development has done better when emphasizing the Christian disciplines associated with Christian growth. But sometimes, the focus is too much on methodology, which though important, might cause us to miss out on their end purpose. Have you ever congratulated yourself that you prayed or read the Bible that day, but found it didn't bring much renewal to your life? In this instance, ritual replaced the needed renewal.

Encouraging believers to grow is much like telling them that they will reach their destination if they just keep driving. At first, they are very excited about getting in the car and starting off on the journey. But gradually, after driving on and on, and not having reached their goal, they begin to lose focus and ask "Why am I doing this?"

Christian training and education has done very poorly in identifying where believers are going and how to get there (and I do not mean heaven). The Lord made these fundamental truths so simple and communicable. Why is the church so ineffectual in passing them on? The church is writhing in unnecessary ignorance and purposelessness, even though God's Word can be easily read and studied.

WHY CAN'T WE TEACH THEM?

It's time we not only learn but pass on what is so important to having a full and abundant Christian life. Jesus said in John 10:10, "I came that they might have life, and might have it abundantly." Peter said, "He Himself bore our sins in His body on the cross, so that we might die to sin and live to righteousness; for by His wounds you were healed" (1 Peter 2:24).

Lessons

- God wants us to understand these truths and therefore built them into His creation.
- Jesus and scripture writers used analogies including the term 'life' to help us grasp and understand important truths for our Christian lives.
- The church as a whole has never really grasped this concept of life and its purpose.
- Christian educational institutions have hidden the most important truths from their students, paralyzing not only their lives but consequentially much of the church.

Memorize & Meditate

John 1:4

John 10:10

Assignment

➡ Do your best to describe spiritual life and how one grows spiritually.

➡ What is the goal of Christian life? Be as specific as possible.

➡ Do you see people finding the abundance of Christian living in their lives? Explain your answer.

➡ What problems have been perpetuated because of unclear teaching about the development of spiritual life and its fullness? Explain why.

#5 The Thrust of Life

Simple is best! Again and again, it has been proven that the simplest is best. This is true for training in spiritual growth too!

God has instilled the most important truths of life through principles that are easily seen in creation. This is the reason Jesus could use simple parables from creation to describe otherwise unclear spiritual truths. The creation, for example, provides a very clear picture of spiritual growth. Although spiritual life is hard to describe due to its spiritual nature, we know many things about its start and development.

Think for a moment about how we actually live: Have you ever seen a parent that gets up early every morning, rushes to their child's side and says, "Grow, grow, grow!"? That would be ridiculous, but not because we do not want them to grow. Any parent is concerned if their child is not properly growing. The reason we don't do this is that we know growth comes naturally, that is, without our planning, encouragement, or obsessive worry. Growth is part of life. Life knows how to develop and grow all on its own.

The same is true with spiritual life. Once present, one can easily see its self determination to grow. No one has to come along and say to the Christian, "Grow, grow, grow!" This would not help the believer to grow, but it could certainly confuse them.

Life's presence

The Spirit of God is connected to these images of life because the Spirit is life. "The Spirit gives life" (2 Corinthians 3:6). Spiritual life appears in the believer when the Holy Spirit begins that new life (Romans 5:5). Once the Holy Spirit comes to dwell in the believer, he or she is set on a path of development and expression. Just like physical growth, the goal is not affirmation of its existence, but the development of maturity.

When believers realize this, fears about their spiritual growth can be set aside. The Holy Spirit's presence in the believers assure them that the power to bring spiritual life to maturity is there in its fullness. Instead of worrying whether they can grow due to past or even ongoing failures, they can delight in God's purpose to grow them and look for ways He will accomplish His goals.

Faith replaces worry. Anticipation supplants lack of direction. The excitement begins as we focus on God's work that He started in our lives when we were saved. This is where renewal begins–at the initiation of our faith. This is not only true for the individual believer but those training God's people. The teachers also must acknowledge God's supernatural power and seek God's supernatural work in the believers.

What God has begun, He will continue. If He has given us new life, then it is meant to grow and develop during our time on earth. "For I am confident of this very thing, that He who began a good work in you will perfect it until the day of Christ Jesus" (Philippians 1:6).

Insights on spiritual life

We must draw some simple but powerful conclusions from this. Some wonder why believers often are not growing spiritually. The problem with spiritual growth is not usually its quality. Just like in physical life, we are either alive or not. A person never says, "I'm not alive enough," though health problems could certainly affect one's quality of life.

When one has been genuinely born again, his or her spiritual life is present, full of potential, and prepared for growth.

Spiritual life is the same for all. We need only to make sure that life is present, and then we should have confidence that life will seek its full development, step by step. There are not different qualities or grades of spiritual life. We should not conclude that the pastor has an intrinsically better quality of spiritual life than us.

Christians may grow at different paces, but this is not due to the power or source of life. There are other reasons for this.

Lessons

- Believers do not need to 'make' themselves grow as if it were unnatural or uncommon. Spiritual life inherently seeks to grow and develop in the lives of all genuine believers.

- There are not different degrees or qualities of God's life; God lives equally in each believer.

- Renewal begins as our hearts express their appreciation to God for His desire to live, grow and work in and through our physical and spiritual lives.

Memorize & Meditate

Philippians 1:6

2 Corinthians 3:6

Assignment

➡ Only genuine believers are born again (same as "born from above"). Are you sure you are born again, i.e., know God through forgiveness of sin found in Jesus Christ's death on the cross? Explain.

➡ Draw a dot. Then write the date and time, to the best of recollection of when you became a believer. This is the time when spiritual life began in you. Then form a ray by drawing an arrow to the right. This arrow signifies God's specially designated growth He is planning to bring about in your life.

➡ Read Ephesians 1:13-14. Note how the Holy Spirit indwells each genuine believer. Thank the Lord for His work in you.

#6 Signs of New Life

Spiritual life, then, much like physical life is a subtle but powerful force inherent in every Christian believer. We need to make sure we have that spiritual life. Remember that Jesus warns us that there is a fundamental difference between the tares and the wheat, or those that have no real genuine life from God and those who do (Matthew 13:24-30).

New life signs

Early on, that difference is nearly impossible to detect. I suppose that is true with physical life too, hidden away in the womb. But there are signs we can look for that affirm the presence of life. A sonograph can show an unborn child's features and movement within the womb, assuring an expecting mother of her child's health. If this is true in the womb, it certainly is true outside it too.

Soon after the birth of our children, our midwife would give an Apgar test to the child, measuring its health by examining the infant's color, breathing, pulse rate, reflex, and muscle tone. All these depict the presence of physical life.

In the physical world we describe movements of large masses, such as water or the atmosphere, as currents or winds. They are large enough that one can readily feel and see them. The visible clouds sail along high above much like a leaf drifting along with the river's current.

Jesus compares the movement of the Spirit of God to both the wind and water. John 3 refers to the wind, "The wind blows where it wishes and you hear the sound of it, but do not know where it comes from and where it is going; so is everyone who is born of the Spirit" (John 3:8). In John 4 Jesus uses flowing water to help us better understand spiritual life.

"But whoever drinks of the water that I shall give him shall never thirst; but the water that I shall give him shall become in him a well of water springing up to eternal life" (John 4:14).

These analogies capture certain insights about the inherent force within life, each speaking of life's majestic power along with its direction. Jesus described the Spirit in John 3 to be similar to the wind blowing this or that way. The force is focused rather than dispersed, and so it is with spiritual life-abounding and free, yet very purposeful.

Expressions of the Spirit's work

John 3:8 states clearly that the believer is "born of the Spirit." His spiritual life is identified with the presence of God's Spirit. Spiritual life, then, has its own 'signs of life' that are fully connected to the Holy Spirit's presence. Here are a few signs of this new life generated by the Spirit.

- A desire for God's Word
- A longing to be with other Christian believers
- A desire to talk to God (prayer)
- An awareness of one's sins
- A desire to turn away from sin
- A need for forgiveness through Jesus Christ
- A growing affection for God and His ways
- An awareness of others and care for their needs

This list could go on, but we have enumerated these to emphasize that the new life in Christ expresses itself through some basic desires and knowledge, just as a newborn baby breathes, moves, cries, and hungers.

The test of life

Jesus said, "Bring forth fruit in keeping with repentance!" (Matthew 3:8) What did He mean? Jesus was simply saying that if they professed to live before God, then there should be signs of life evident in them. In this case, they would be aware of their sins and be humbled by them. Instead of treating people wrongly, they would care for them. There are many signs of new life, some are more apparent than others. These desires stem from the new life birthed by the Holy Spirit deep in our hearts. They will shape our thinking and behavior as time goes on and thus will make our spiritual growth evident to others.

Lessons

- Wind and rivers teach us about the presence, purpose, and power of the Holy Spirit.
- New life comes from the Spirit's presence in our soul.
- Spiritual life, like physical life, reveals its genuineness through certain expected signs.

- These signs of spiritual life will always be present in a genuine believer, though they can be repressed or damaged by continuing in sin.

Memorize & Meditate

Matthew 3:8

1 John 3:10, 23-24

Assignment

➡ Think about when you first came to know Jesus. Review the signs of life listed above. Can you observe them in your own life? Write down the most significant ones.

-
-
-
-

➡ What about today? These signs should still be there. Yes, temptations and drifting from the Lord will suppress them, but what is most important to you? If any of these signs of life mentioned above are true of you, write them next to the diagram below.

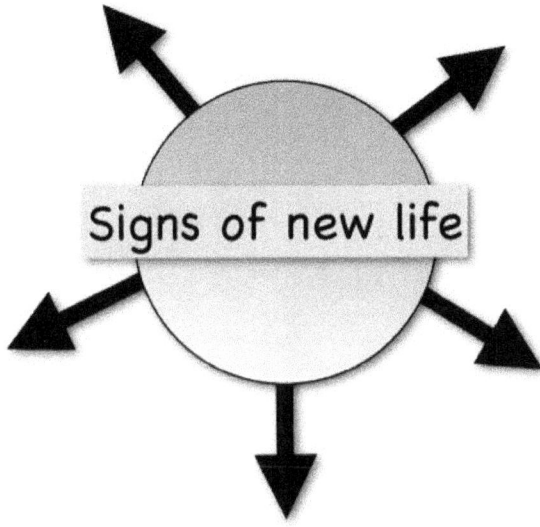

Signs of new life

➡ After writing them down, state each one aloud in a prayer such as, "I love your Word, Lord." These are deep desires that are now true of you, whether you have perfectly expressed them or not. (Praying them is very important!)

➡ If these desires are not true of you, then more than likely you still do not have the Spirit of life in you. You need to come to know the Lord. Call on the Lord to save you through Jesus Christ.

➡ Study John 3:1-8 and John 4:10-14 as time permits. Find the key phrases that connect the Spirit with wind or water, reminding us that the Holy Spirit is the source of eternal life.

#7 Life's Source

Spiritual life, then, much like physical life is a powerful force inherent in every Christian believer. Once acknowledged, the new life begins to express itself through many different means.

Born of the Spirit

This life, like a powerful flowing current, is focused and guided. This life force does not, for example, bring us to think wrong of others. This is because the source of this force is the Holy Spirit; we are "born of God."[3]

---

3 Not wanting to get too technical here, but the contrast is interesting. John three mentions being born of the Spirit while 1 John uses the phrase, "born of God" seven times, illustrating John's understanding that the Spirit is co-equal with God.

Jesus says that we are born again or born from above. "Jesus answered, 'Truly, truly, I say to you, unless one is born of water and the Spirit, he cannot enter into the kingdom of God. That which is born of the flesh is flesh, and that which is born of the Spirit is spirit'" (John 3:5-6). Our new life's powerful force is sourced in God Himself. This new life then is the same as the Holy Spirit living His life through our lives. This is the reason the scriptures commonly refer to the believer as having a 'new life in the spirit' or Spirit (from the same Greek word in the Bible).

The Spirit of God working in us

This understanding is important because through it we can see the ways the Spirit of God always helps us. He wants to make us more like the Father, so He exerts his power pursuant of this goal (He is not just an impersonal force but is God Himself). Similarly, the Spirit will not use His power to cause us to do wrong, evil, or anything contrary to His good and holy purpose.

Most of our Christian life will be characterized by identifying what the Holy Spirit wants to do in and through our lives. In faith, we day by day carry them out.

The Spirit's power is mighty. We can never tame it (i.e., Him) nor successfully counter it, though we can grieve Him

(Ephesians 4:30). Our best hope, like the white water rafters, is to put all our efforts at staying on course along the mighty Spirit's course.

Lessons

- The Holy Spirit is the source of our new life force, inspiring us and providing strength to do all that God wants.
- We do not need to be strong on our own. We are like those manning the rafts and need to focus on carrying out what God the Spirit wants for our lives.

Memorize & Meditate

John 3:5-6

1 John 5:1,4

Assignment

➡ Name three things the Holy Spirit wants you to do.

-
-
-

➡ Say a prayer to God. Thank Him for giving you the desire to please Him and carry out these things. Ask God for special wisdom, strength, and help so that through the Spirit's aid you will rightly carry these actions out for God's glory.

#8 Catch the Spirit

A powerful river's current is one way to picture the flowing force in a believer's life. Strong wind currents also help us understand these invisible forces. Although storms may have gusty winds, they are comprised of huge flowing currents that are part of a larger system. The winds have direction and operate within certain parameters.

Strong currents

These strong currents help us think more clearly about the Holy Spirit's work in our lives. First, we must, as communicated in the last chapter, remember that God is carrying out His purposes. In the middle of a storm, we might feel confused as to the direction the wind is blowing. We need not worry, however. God is in control, even when wicked forces arise. Our duty is to affirm God's greater purposes and play our small but important part. Affirm that you want to be used for God's purposes no matter how difficult circumstances appear. Remember too that we have all the strength we need to carry out God's purposes. We need to both affirm our desire to please God but also to rely on His strength.

The uplift of the wind provides a picture of how we need God's Spirit to help us. Eagles have powerful wings but need rising air currents or "thermals" to go under those wings and lift them up.

> "Yet those who wait for the LORD Will gain new strength; They will mount up with wings like eagles, They will run and not get tired, They will walk and not become weary" (Isaiah 40:31).

I have a friend who hang glides high in the sky (see his picture above). I wouldn't want to do that! We have a choice of whether to hang glide or not, but not with living along with the Spirit of God. The question is, "How conscious are we of God's purposeful work in our lives?" Many believers' faith at this point blur into a, "I don't know what God is doing in my life."

Impossible steps of life

The Spirit always lead us to do God's will. Sometimes this will lead us into paths that will seem impossible. Why might they seem impossible?

- Physically beyond our abilities
- Insufficient time
- Financially beyond our means
- Opposition by family and friends
- Inadequate abilities or giftings

• Lack of self-confidence

The list could go on! The Spirit, however, will at times lead us into such difficult circumstances. Have you experienced a difficult person? Sure. You can be sure that He will also give patience or whatever is needed to love him. This is an earmark of God's way—asking us to go beyond our natural abilities so that we will learn to rely on Him.

We often tend to go along with our natural tendencies, depending on our personalities and instincts. Some people will brave anything–much like Peter. They don't always come out successfully, however. Others are much more timid, like Thomas. Doubt will cause them to give up easily.

Our point is not to show you here how to work with the Spirit of God but to highlight the way He works. We need to learn how to rely on His help. (See our book on the second level of discipleship to better understand the dynamics of spiritual growth and warfare: *Reaching Beyond Mediocrity*). Only God has the strength, wisdom, and insight to know how to accomplish His will, especially when facing a clever enemy like the devil who seeks our demise.

Keep focused and alert

Jesus said, "Keep watching and praying, that you may not enter into temptation; the spirit is willing, but the flesh is weak" (Matthew 26:41). The genuine believer has the desire to please God, but somehow we tend to fall into temptations when we do not see how God can clearly help us handle a particular situation. We not only need to focus on the Lord in prayer to discern what He wants but also to learn how to gain faith, strength, and wisdom from Him. When we start praying we may not have any of these needed items. As we come to Him in prayer, however, He gives them to us.

The love for the things of God and the willingness to embrace the things of God are all from the Holy Spirit. They are implanted in us when we initially trust Christ for salvation and are born again. We don't need to contrive or produce these feelings on our own. The new believer can worship God as deeply as the experienced Christian. We don't need to struggle to develop those desires, Confusion, however, may come upon us when we question what we love, who we are, and what we should be doing. Acquiring the truth of God clarifies our true selves in Christ, while the evil one attempts to negatively manipulate how we think of ourselves.

God is our strength! That powerful wind is carrying us along as we abide by His principles and call on Him for help.

Lessons

- God wants us to rely on Him for wisdom, time, opportunities, and other things to get His work done.
- The Lord eagerly seeks to give us what we need to carry out His will, but we tend to rely on our own resources that will eventually fail us.
- Sometimes we confront impossible people and situations, but the Lord is always there to help us succeed, even if a miracle is needed.

Memorize & Meditate

Matthew 26:41

Psalm 5:3, Isaiah 40:31

Assignment

➡ In what ways do you tend to rely on your own resources to carry out God's work but get frustrated and fail?

-

-

➡ What kind of personality do you have? How might that shape how you try to get through difficult circumstances?

➡ Keeping Matthew 26:41 in mind, do you "watch and pray" only when facing what you think are difficult situations, or also as a daily spiritual discipline? Explain.

(2) Appreciate the Life Core

Chapters 9-18

#9 Becoming Aware

Making Connections

Having stated how the Spirit generally works, we need to look at His work from a personal view. Later in the last section of the book, we will yet take another view from the educator or trainers' point of view.

In physical life, we are often unaware of life's presence. Although driven by and totally affected by this powerful life force, we somehow are oblivious to its daily life-giving properties.

Oblivious to life

At puberty young men and women are very conscious of the changes their bodies are undergoing. Though giving full attention to their changing bodies and interests, they hardly ever think about the life which brings about those changes. As a result, young people tend to pay much attention to who they are. Later in life, people tend to focus more on what they have.

Few, however, contemplate the reason they are able to grow into adults or later able to get a job. The busyness of day-to-day living masks our understanding and awareness of our physical and spiritual lives.

Our ignorance and lack of attention to God's life, the all-empowering breath He breathed into us, makes us unappreciative of the mystery of life. Unthankfulness leads to autonomous living ,which in turn, breeds a sense of arrogance.

This is the heartbeat of today's materialistic and secular age. With the belief that all is defined by chemicals and matter, there is no longer the impetus to look at the power behind their lives. They easily block out thoughts of God's involvement in the affairs of this world, though they literally depend upon Him for everything they have.

A hidden spiritual problem

This ignorance has affected the church too, but on another level. We are inattentive of the life-giving force behind our spiritual lives. We tend to focus much more on what we can see and touch rather than on what enables our sight and devotion.

There have been moves of God during my lifetime that have refreshed the church. The book, *Body Life*, by Ray Stedman made God's people conscious of spiritual gifts as well as the Spirit of God that empowers His people with these gifts The connection between the two was both practical and theologically right on. God's people were blessed, but this brief development was short and hidden behind other theological developments.

The charismatic movement, in a similar way, has connected spiritual gifts with the Holy Spirit but expanded in a great swath stretching across the globe. People started having Bible studies and prayer meetings even in lifeless churches. Regardless of one's view of these gifts, and certainly there was an overemphasis on signs in some places, this renewed attention upon the Spirit's work in our life brought life back into dead churches and organizations.

The more we disconnect the awareness of God's living Spirit abiding in us from our Christian lives, the more spiritually dead we will become. Knowing about a church does not make us a church member, nor does knowing much about God make us know God. It is good if we know these things, but the neglect of emphasis on God's central place in our lives or training can become a major stumbling block. This spiritual blindness is called unbelief and always keeps us from securing victory.

Revivals of old

Previous revivals restored this awareness of the presence of God. People humbly admitted it was not their great attempts to know God, but the Spirit of God working in and through them that made such a difference in their lives. This consciousness of God's Spirit actively working through our lives remains fundamental. When ignored, distortions arise including religiosity, theological pride, spiritual boredom, and lowered moral standards. They all result in not being clear how God works in and through our lives.

The resulting belief ends up being cousins to religious humanism. The focus is on man's effort and thought rather than on God. This is exactly what we see in our 'anthrocentric' (lit. man-centered) world today.

Practical atheism

I have used the term 'practical atheism' to describe believers who conduct their Christian lives without being aware of God's presence. The Psalmist cautioned God's people not to live like the people who are driven by their appetites—like the beasts of the field. "Man in his pomp, yet without understanding, is like the beasts that perish" (Psalm 49:20).

Christians face a great danger of living without a true awareness of God's presence animating their lives. God is behind the scenes, but the believer can go along without any real consciousness of this. The same is true for those serving God. They can preach, teach, and evangelize but be unaware of the Spirit's inner work. We must ask, "Is God really part of their belief system?" Can their religious activities be carried out without God? If so, does it not reveal its true identify of being man-made than God-made?

This constant awareness of God's work in the believer—think faith—must return to the church. It is not just a person giving, going to church, or helping the poor. We live in God's presence, and He is carrying out His good purposes through our lives.

> *The fool has said in his heart, "There is no God." They are corrupt, they have committed abominable deeds; There is no one who does good. The LORD has looked down from heaven upon the sons of men, to see if there are any who understand, who seek after God.*
>
> *They have all turned aside; together they have become corrupt; There is no one who does good, not even one. 4 Do all the workers of wickedness not know, who eat up my people as they eat bread, And do not call upon the LORD? (Psalm 14:1-4).*

Seeking His presence

Revival comes at times when we again are willing to restore the proper place of God in our lives. As long as we are self-reliant, we operate from our own resources and little or no glory goes to God. When we, however, become desperate, we call on Him. When we become aware of His presence and experience His answered prayer, then true worship begins.

This is how God uses difficult times in our lives to rejuvenate us (Psalm 119:23-24). What would happen, however, if we

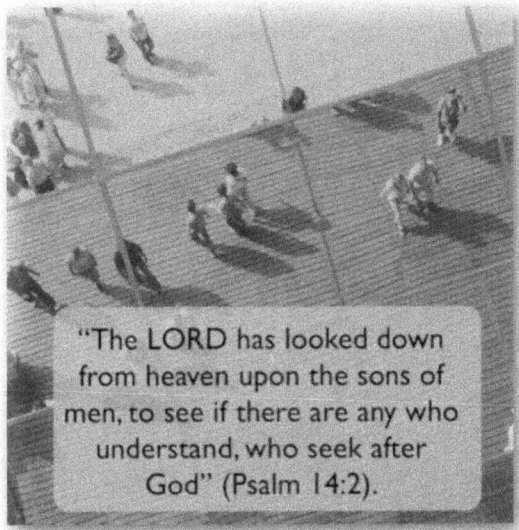

"The LORD has looked down from heaven upon the sons of men, to see if there are any who understand, who seek after God" (Psalm 14:2).

regularly sought His face rather than having to be poked and prodded by trials?

Our society as a whole has begun to think about life as if God is not at work. This same worldly thinking has seeped into the church where we see less and less difference between the world and the professing believer.

Lessons

- Mankind, including many professing Christians, live unaware of God's physical and spiritual life-giving forces.

- Without a consciousness of God's work in our lives, our hearts become hardened and arrogance grows.

- When we focus on the presence of God in our lives, then we are humbled, appreciative, God–centered and properly dependent on Him.

Memorize & Meditate

Psalm 14:1-2

Philippians 3:17-19

Assignment

➡ Examine your life for signs of autonomy from God. Do you live your Christian life or carry out your ministry without a sense of God's help and guidance in what you are or do? Explain.

➡ Evaluate the consciousness of those around you (church and non–churched) of God's active presence. For the Christians, do they pray or commune with God? Is God speaking through His Word to them or are they just reading it?

#10 Welcoming

When God is alive in our hearts and minds, we constantly seek His presence. John says this in a curious way in the first chapter of his Gospel. He first speaks about this Life (1:4) that came into the world and identifies this Life and Light as Jesus Christ in John 1:14.

The preceding verses are intriguing: "But as many as received Him, to them He gave the right to become children of God, even to those who believe in His name, who were born not of blood, nor of the will of the flesh, nor of the will of man, but of God" (John 1:12-13). Those that receive Him are the ones to whom God gave His new life. God birthed His Spirit in them and brought that new life into existence.

Being a gracious host

These are the ones that receive or welcome Him. The Greek word used is the same as a host who would greet and welcome a person into his or her home.

What a difference between the person who welcomes and entertains his guest and the one who doesn't even recognize the guest's presence. God is not just living around us as an energy force. The Lord is a person, and we actively entertain and please Him, making Him feel at home. Strong Christian lives cultivate an ongoing relationship with the Lord through the Spirit.

Seeking the Lord

Being consciousness of God's presence, then, is followed up by a heart that welcomes and seeks Him. The phrase 'seek Him' is used many times in the scripture but is rather intangible. I have meditated on it many times, trying to grasp its meaning and full implication.

'Seeking the Lord' is built upon the fact that God is there. This is where faith comes into the picture because we cannot see Him. "And without faith it is impossible to please Him, for he who comes to God must believe that He is, and that He is a **rewarder of those who seek Him**" (Hebrews 11:6).

Faith is the backbone of the Christian life and a critical expression of its life. With faith, there is life. Without faith, there is no spiritual life. God said of King Rehoboam, "He did evil because he did not set his heart to seek the LORD" (2 Chronicles 12:14).

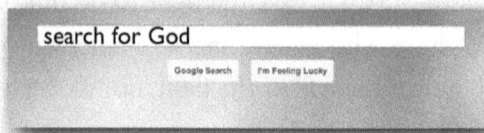

search for God

Google Search   I'm Feeling Lucky

When a person seeks God, there is not only an awareness of God but the desire to know and please Him. Our searching for Him is an expression of those desires to know Him and His will. We want to know Him and learn of His ways. We desire to be closer to Him and participate in what He does.

A good host makes his guest feel at home. The guest is made part of the host's life and home for that period. For a Christian believer, this personal relationship with God never ends. After Jesus Christ moves into the heart of the believer, he increasingly searches out how to specially treat this Guest in his life.

Lessons

• The believer not only initially welcomes Jesus into His life at its beginning (i.e., salvation) but throughout his life continually seeks to deepen his awareness of Christ Jesus who now lives in him.

• Faith arises from that new nature that God gives us. A growing faith represents our conscious acknowledgement and welcome of God's presence and work in our lives.

Memorize & Meditate

Hebrews 11:6

John 1:12-13

Assignment

➡ Return your thoughts to when God first opened your heart to respond to Him. Reflect on John 1:12-13 and how you, then, opened your heart to Him.

➡ Search the phrase 'seek the Lord' in the Bible. Make two or three observations about these verses or its usage.

➡ Think about your past week. In what ways, have you sought out the Lord? How important was it to you?
Not much..... Little.....Much? Explain.

#11 A Growing Faith

The way that we acknowledge, seek, and pursue the Lord has a lot to do with our Christian growth. These actions describe spiritual growth itself, just as growing taller, maturing, and getting stronger are indicators of physical growth.

Two challenges

Believers who seek the Lord's presence use and thus strengthen their faith. Those that are not seeking Him are not living by faith, but drop back to living by sight.

Christians have two major challenges, each requiring one to use his or her faith:

(1) Learning how to return to the Lord when he or she has fallen.

(2) Consistently pursuing the Lord even when all is well.

In both cases, faith is needed. When a believer humbles his heart, combined with a genuine confession, he exercises his faith in the Lord as he seeks Him.

King Rehoboam, unlike his father Solomon, did not begin his rule well. He adopted ideas from his friends rather than wise advisors. The kingdom split as a result. But despite that setback, when he did seek the Lord, he was blessed—but this blessing sadly took place only after those wasted years when he turned away from the Lord.

When the kingdom of Rehoboam was established and strong, he and all Israel with him forsook the law of the Lord (2 Chr 12:1).

The Lord, however, turned away from chastising Rehoboam when he again sought the Lord. "And when he humbled himself, the anger of the LORD turned away from him, so as not to destroy him completely; and also conditions were good in Judah (2 Chr 12:12).

Pieces of the puzzle

These principles of how God deals with His people are important for us to learn. But it is equally critical to connect what we are experiencing with a picture of God's whole training scheme. This enables us to more quickly grasp a clear picture of how God is dealing with us and how to improve our lives.

Our spiritual welfare is dependent upon our faith, what we believe about God in 'real time'. When our faith is strong, then our spiritual life grows. When it is weak, then we struggle with spiritual defeat.

The strength of our faith is not dependent on our past record or whether we're currently doing good or bad. Remember, it was when Rehoboam was doing well that he fell. When he was broken, he sought the Lord. Our spiritual well-being is dependent on how we presently respond to the Lord.

This explains why we can fall when everything seems to be going fine or when we're down. In brokenness, we can call on

Spiritual growth
Growing faith

Spiritual decline
Diminishing faith

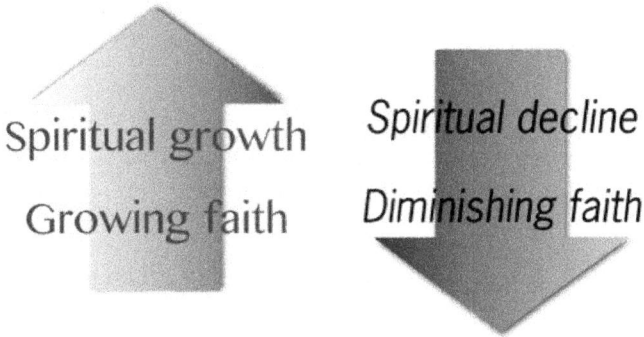

God for special help and find it. Our strength depends on our present faith.

God wants us to avoid spiritual failure and to remain strong. The scriptures regularly exhort us to be strong. A strong faith must master the ins and outs of temptation and learn how to steady one's focus on staying strong in one's faith. Meditating on each scenario and how one seeks the Lord will further fortify one's faith. Our growing faith is closely tied to affirming the importance of God and His work so that it shapes our decisions. Spiritual weakness is connected to the lack of belief that the Lord is important to one or more areas of our lives.

These changes and opportunities take place secretly in our hearts and minds. In the next chapter, we will better understand how a thriving life from God is dependent upon certain growing conditions. God is allowing circumstances to drive us closer and closer to Him.

Lessons

- Spiritual growth stems from exercising our faith or trust in God.
- Spiritual defeat results from no longer sincerely believing God's way is important or best.

Memorize & Meditate

2 Chronicles 2:12

2 Chronicles 2:1-14

Assignment

➡ Describe your faith in God. As you do, rate how important you think God is in your life on a scale from 0 to 10.

➡ Think of a time when you were backsliding. Describe your doubts at that time. Were you doubting some aspect of God or His ways?

#12 Our Life Goals

The Holy Spirit is that spiritual life within us

Every force has directionality and strength. For instance, the wind might blow towards the Northeast at sixty miles per hour. That would be a strong wind!

The hidden powers

Our life force is the same. Our physical bodies grow due according to this life force which enables us to function in this busy, modern world. We can speak on cell phones or hop off a busy bus stuffed with people. The spiritual life force thoroughly infuses our physical lives. Though it largely works through our physical frame and mind, it has its own power and purpose.

In order for us to grow, we need to better discern the direction or goals of this spiritual life. Instead of working counter to our spiritual life goals, we ought to work along with them. I have walked the streets of Chicago on very windy days where it took great effort to move. The wind was blowing against me. On the other hand, I have also been moving along on a bicycle at a great pace without pedaling because a strong wind was pushing me from behind. Are you working with the Spirit?

Broadening our knowledge

Knowledge remains a key aspect in our spiritual growth. If we could combine that awareness of what God is doing in our lives and commit our will to it, then most of our spiritual struggles would disappear.

The fact is, though, many believers are rather ignorant about what goals God has for them. Some of this is natural. As we peer through our windows at the street, we do not see spiritual things. We might see people, cars, trees, or sidewalks, but rarely do we ever get a glimpse of angels and demons. Like the wind, the Spirit of God cannot be seen with our eyes. We only see how He impacts things in the real world. The wind blows the tops of the trees back and forth.

Elisha's servant's eyes had to be open to see the spiritual world. "Then Elisha prayed and said, "O LORD, I pray, open his eyes that he may see." And the LORD opened the servant's eyes, and he saw; and behold, the mountain was full of horses and chariots of fire all around Elisha" (2 Kings 6:17).

Through the study of God's Word, we can begin to gain a feel of the spiritual world. For example, we know from the Book of Hebrews that at least one angel stands over each child of God (Hebrews 1:14).

The wind is blowing

God's Word doesn't speak much about these curious details, but it does illuminate much about the essentials—what He's doing through the spiritual life force in us. Paul has identified this goal for believers:

And we proclaim Him (Christ), admonishing every man and teaching every man with all wisdom, that we may present every man complete in Christ (Colossians 1:28).

Peter says it slightly differently, "But like the Holy One who called you, be holy yourselves also in all your behavior; because it is written, 'You shall be holy, for I am holy'" (1 Peter 1:15-16).

'Complete in Christ' and 'holy' are just two ways of describing the direction of the spiritual life 'winds' acting upon our lives.

We have been using the term 'spiritual life force' in comparison to our physical life force to help us understand it better, but there is much more to all of this. Just as Christ through His Word creates and sustains physical life (Col 1:15-17), so Christ through the Spirit provides that 'life force' within us.

One of the troubles we get into as believers is the assumption that physical life and spiritual life just happen. This is not true. God's forces are at work in us to complete His will. This is true for every person and created thing. All things are made to bring glory to God. This is also true with the Holy Spirit that imparts spiritual life to those believing in Christ.

And I will ask the Father, and He will give you another Helper, that He may be with you forever; that is the Spirit of truth, whom the world cannot receive, because it does not behold Him or know Him, but you know Him because He abides with you, and will be in you (John 14:16-17).

God is alive in us to empower our spiritual awareness, to commune with us, so that as a team we can accomplish His glorious purposes in and through our lives.

Lessons

- The 'spiritual life force' is analogous to the 'physical life force' driving our human bodies.
- The spiritual life force at work in our lives is the same as Christ working in us through the Holy Spirit.
- When we consciously join our wills with God's purpose of working, in both our physical and spiritual lives, living out our spiritual lives becomes much easier and focused.

Memorize & Meditate

1 Peter 1:15-16

John 14:16-17

Assignment

➡ Have you thought about God using His Holy Spirit in you to accomplish His purposes? Explain.

➡ Just from Colossians 1:28 and 1 Peter 1:15-16, what would you say God is trying to do through the spiritual life force within you? How far along are you?

#13 Seeking Direction

God actively lives in us to help us be Christ-like. This is a wonderful and amazing truth, but we can still get confused. (The evil one works double time to make sure we run into confusion.) Believers may become perplexed as to what it means to live out a Christ-like life or may even just see it as an impossibility, something to be reserved for heaven.

They face all sorts of spiritual struggles and do not know how to overcome them. Maybe these believers, as an example, don't know how to properly handle personal relationships. They get bitter and upset with others. They end up being anything but loving.

When we see a little baby, we do not place on them expectations associated with an adult. That would be crazy. Babies can't even feed themselves! That will come, but it takes time. And so it is with spiritual life.

Another helpful life analogy

John used physical life as an analogy to help us understand both the existence and essence of spiritual life (as we discussed from

John, chapters 1, 3 & 5). He has provided us another very helpful analogy that clarifies the development of our spiritual lives.

Human spiritual life develops in a similar way to human physical life. No doubt there are differences, but overall the similarities allow us to gain great insight into the development of spiritual life at different stages in the Christian life. This analogy is so helpful that when I have difficulty grasping some aspect of spiritual life, I often look at what is happening in our physical lives at that stage to gain insight.

In 1 John 2:12-14 John provides for us the key to understand the three levels of spiritual life. These three spiritual stages of life simply and yet profoundly deepen our understanding of the spiritual life process. What seems to be conceptual or hidden, now becomes practical and clear.

1 John 2:12-14

I am writing to you, little children, because your sins are forgiven you for His name's sake. I am writing to you, fathers, because you know Him who has been from the beginning. I am writing to you, young men, because you have overcome the evil one.

I have written to you, children, because you know the Father. I have written to you, fathers, because you know Him who has been from the beginning. I have written to you, young men, because you are strong, and the word of God abides in you, and you have overcome the evil one (1 John 2:12-14).

The phrases 'children,' 'young men,' and 'fathers' are familiar and powerful images. I have had people challenge me as to whether this really applies to spiritual growth because of the emphasis on physical development and age. As we look more closely at the descriptions attached to each category, however,

John is obviously referring to spiritual characteristics rather than physical ones. "Overcome the evil one" and "word of God abides in you" clearly are not referring to physical life but spiritual life.

Only three stages

In the fields of developmental (biological) psychology, we have learned many things about physical development. Each of these three areas of development will be mentioned briefly, but the focus will be kept on how they fit into spiritual life as a whole. (We have other training materials that are devoted to explaining and applying these truths to each of the three stages.)

The spiritual life force derived by the Holy Spirit relentlessly drives the followers of Jesus Christ toward transformation into the full image of Christ.

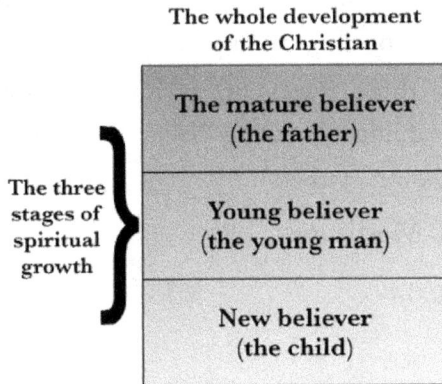

**The whole development
of the Christian**

The three
stages of
spiritual
growth }

**The mature believer
(the father)**

**Young believer
(the young man)**

**New believer
(the child)**

The three stages help clarify what is supposed to happen at each of these stages. As we facilitate this growth, believers will grow strong. When and where we ignore our responsibilities to help ourselves or other believers grow, faith will weaken.

Sources of confusion and strength

As we look at our churches today, we should not blame the Word of God or God Himself for the confusion or purposeless found in the church. The church herself has neglected her responsibility to make disciples. Our hope is, however, that when we get serious on being like Christ and obeying what Christ has commanded, the church will again grow strong. Jesus' followers, like the disciples of old, will carry out His work in His love.

God chose to impress this developmental path in our minds by using one of the most common pictures of growing up in our families to instruct us. In the succeeding chapters, we will highlight the way these stages help us focus on helping believers, ourselves, or others grow.

Lessons

- The spiritual development of believers has many similarities to the physical development of human beings.
- Weakness in the church has nothing to do with the lack of power of the gospel or God's Word, but the failure of God's people to responsibly train up those around them.
- There are three stages of spiritual development: new believers (children), young believers (young men) and mature believers (fathers).

Memorize & Meditate

1 John 2:12-14

Assignment

➡ Study 1 John 2:12-14. What three groups do you find? Highlight one difference for each stage, both physically and spiritually.

➡ In what order has John discussed them?

➡ Are you aware of anyone being discipled? If not, why do you think this is the case?

#14 Curiosity

Where am I?
Where should I be?
How can I get there?

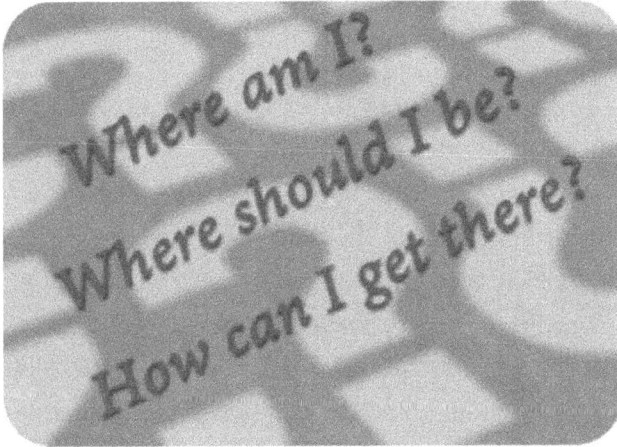

Once believers learn about these three stages, and realize there is no fourth stage, they begin to wonder about which group they fit into. It is much like showing a group photo at a picnic or outing. Our eyes tend to scan the picture for ourselves. Am I in the picture? What do I look like?

Christians, filled with curiosity about their own lives, want to know how far along they have come. Most believers have never even heard of these levels of spiritual development so it sparks some interest even in those who have a lukewarm faith. The Lord also used family analogies that every believer could easily understand, embrace, and pass on to others.

When speaking of levels, there is the danger that one person will perceive himself greater or more important than another, and even think that he needs to set others straight (you could call them spiritual bullies). This is hardly the purpose that John has in mind.

Instead of comparing ourselves with others, we should seek to identify how far along the Holy Spirit's life force has enabled us to reflect Christ's likeness. This should be reflected in the way we conduct our lives as well as in our services or ministries. This proper interest in our spiritual lives leads us into thinking about how much we have grown and in what other areas we need to further mature. Think of yourself like a little boy that dreams about growing up to be like his Daddy.

A fresh vision of growth needed

Most believers, instead of seeing healthy growth, have fallen into spiritual stagnancy. They are not growing. They do not even know that they are expected to continue growing! Or if they do realize this, they feel defeated. They have troubles in one or more areas of their lives and have largely given up hope that they can be any different from what they presently see in themselves. They think that this is where they will remain.

Much like training a growing vine to where we want it to go, so we need to lead our thoughts. Whenever we combine the understanding of God's powerful life forces along with His specialized purpose for us at each stage of our Christian lives, then we can surge forward in our Christian development.

Just as growth spurts in our physical lives propel us towards adulthood, so in our spiritual lives comprehension of His truths bring increases in faith that cause us to spiritually grow. The chain of thoughts that build up our anticipation of spiritual growth might go something like this:

- The Holy Spirit is still drawing me toward full spiritual development; He hasn't given up on me.

- Hmm, where have I turned down the wrong path?

- God has a plan for me.

- God has equipped me to grow into maturity.

- Where am I at?

- What is the next step for me to grow in?

- How can I grow more?

These are a few of the possible thoughts that are triggered from the proper teaching of God's Word on spiritual life. These truths lead the believer back onto the right track where their faith in God's work in them will be re-ignited.

A growing hope

"You mean you really want me to be like Jesus? Will you help me understand what that practically means for me and will you show me the way there? What is the next step for me?"

These thoughts and questions engender faith—the anticipation that the believer can and should grow more spiritually.

They are now thinking about spiritual development and begin to look at the goals God has for them rather than the problems that they had been facing. The hope of change begins to return. Along with increased faith, they have the promises that God will enable them to keep growing.

A strong confidence in God's plan

Each believer, step by step, is meant to grow up into full maturity through the various stages of spiritual life. Some might object to this teaching, but it is what is being taught here in 1 John 2:12-14. The bigger problem behind our suspicions is our faulty concepts of maturity. No one can become perfect, without sin. Though already stained, we can still see our lives transformed by consistent godly decision making that brings glory to God. Notice how John's words ring with these thoughts:

My little children, I am writing these things to you that you may not sin. And if anyone sins, we have an Advocate with the Father, Jesus Christ the righteous; and He Himself is the propitiation for our sins; and not for ours only, but also for those of the whole world. And by this we know that we have come to know Him, if we keep His commandments (1 John 2:1-3).

"O send out Thy light and Thy truth, let them lead me; Let them bring me to Thy holy hill" (Psalm 42:3).

When believers become curious, they are open to learn and grow (teachers know how important teachability is in their students). It is so different from the mentality of the believer who thinks he has already arrived (whatever that means) by coming to church for fifteen years.

Becoming eager to grow

We do need to make life grow. It grows on its own. Just like a little sprout, we need to protect that little plant and provide it necessary elements such as water, fertilizer, and sunshine. So though, we don't make the life or growth, we do cultivate its growth. So it is with the Christian life.

Once the believer understands his potential for growth, he is eager to acquire more of the truth of God's Word to reshape his mind. Leaving ignorance behind, he exalts in the glory of God's great purposes for him in Christ Jesus.

O send out Thy light and Thy truth, let them lead me; Let them bring me to Thy holy hill, And to Thy dwelling places. Then I will go to the altar of God, To God my exceeding joy; And upon the lyre I shall praise Thee, O God, my God (Psalm 42:3-4).

Growth is possible. When we believe it, like David, we pursue it by faith at whatever level we presently are at in our spiritual lives. Even when in sin, like David, we can by God's grace escape the grasp of evil (Psalm 32).

Lessons

- Stagnated growth is noted by the lack of desire to grow, or the belief that growth is no longer necessary or important.
- If believers see spiritual growth as a real possibility, their interest in growing is reignited.

Memorize & Meditate

Psalm 42:3-4

1 John 2:1-3

Assignment

➡ How eager are people to learn God's Word around you? Evaluate the attitudes of those attending the meetings to learn, pray, and worship.

➡ How enthusiastic are you in learning and growing? In what areas could you be stronger? Do you think you have room for growth in those areas? Explain.

#15 The Child–Stage #1

The Little Child

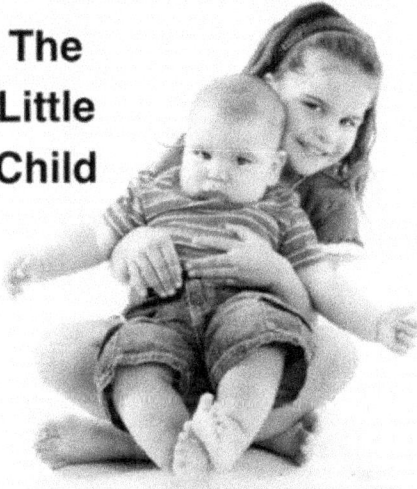

The promises of spiritual growth are hidden in the descriptions of what is to happen at each stage of the Christian life. In this chapter, we look at what God promises to do for the new believer, the little child.

Each of us has started his or her life as a baby, grown through his or her preteen/teen years and then, assuming the reader is older, has stepped into adulthood. The age when one transitions from one stage to another is not all that clear, but the process is.

Growth markers

There are two key growth markers to help us keep track of our growth. The first is our birth along with its celebration. A new baby has entered the world! Proud parents send out an announcement and photos of their new treasure.

The other clear marker is when one has become, in the terms of 1st John, a father. This once small person is now fully grown and has a child of his own. A complete cycle has finally occurred, one generation producing another.

The modern world has tried to redefined adulthood as simply being older and independent, with no requirement for parenthood and its inherent responsibilities. Unfortunately, the church in many ways has also adopted this mentality. This leaves both the society and the church distressed because older believers do not act accountable for the training of younger believers.[4]

A true, full cycle directs the believer not only to become an adult but also to bear fruit and take responsibility for the next generation.

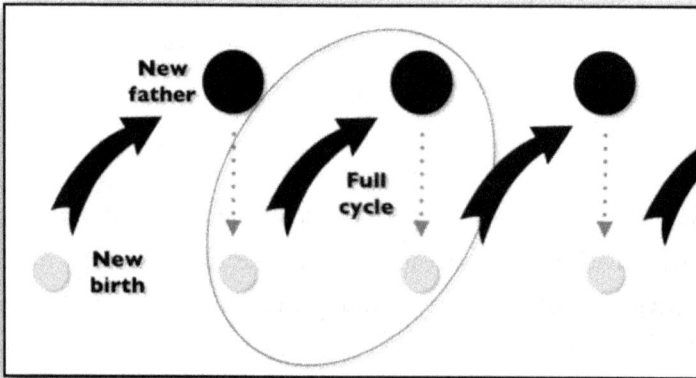

One full cycle: Birth to Fatherhood

This current lesson focuses on the all important first stage where new life begins. John the apostle uses the analogy of our physical development in the family to help us understand our development in God's spiritual family. Like Jesus he uses what is familiar to teach the unfamiliar. In previous chapters, we discussed the importance of new spiritual life. The new believer has a new life and is therefore likened to a baby.

---

[4] So-called 'family planning' should be renamed for what it is 'barren planning.' Societies along with the church are suffering because of this anti-biblical mindset.

The baby grows

Just as a baby must grow through the steps of physical development–crawling, sitting, etc., so God has the new believer learn many basic lessons during this first stage of spiritual development. The stages of life are important because at each stage, the individual is learning or growing in many different ways.

My ten year-old Rebekah convinced me last week to take her and her older brother, Isaac now thirteen, to the playground. They wanted to go to a certain park to play for it held fond memories from previous years. So off the three of us went. After playing for about five or ten minutes, they decided it was not interesting anymore. I overheard them saying, "I guess we are too old for the park, now." They suggested taking a nature hike instead. They greatly enjoyed climbing the hills in the park. People change as they grow.

The little 'spiritual' child has just come to know the Lord. This might be a fifty year-old person, but it doesn't matter. Spiritual birth ushers every believer into the world as a new member of God's family.

Older believers in Christ should grow through this first stage a bit quicker, but it is important to remember they still go through this basic developmental stage. If not rightly cared for, the chances are slim of properly growing in their spiritual lives.

Caring for new believers

When you first became a believer, were you cared for? Did someone give you personal attention? These questions might seem inconsequential, but they are not. Notice the special attention that the baby gains after birth. It is during this time that person, usually the parent, gives this wee little baby one-on-one attention.

Not only is the baby being breast fed, but the baby is being loved, washed, dressed, etc. The schedule might be repetitious and tiring, especially late at night, but it is critical. But notice what is happening. Close to the Mom, the baby has the opportunity to hear loving words, sounds, and expressions. The baby is not only learning how to respond and communicate, but how to love through hugs, fun, and little games the child experiences.

What happens when the baby is scared and starts crying? The Mom rushes to the baby. While holding the baby close to her body, she gently says, "All is well. Don't cry. Mommy has you."

The child is not only mechanically gaining the physical food and attention he or she needs, but just as important, receiving emotional love. This is the ideal situation. On the other hand, if the mother is absent or aloof, the result will be a scarred child who feels unloved. God passes all this responsibility of love, care, and nurturing on to the older believers. If an older believer cares for the new believer as God has planned, that little one will grow strong, but if not, the foundation for that new believer will remain weak.

Lots to learn!

The new believer has many things to learn. Peter also uses an analogy to help us understand new believers. He uses the newborn's desires to help us understand how the new believer loves to acquire the Word of God. It is likened to the believers' milk.

> *"Like newborn babes, long for the pure milk of the word, that by it you may grow in respect to salvation" (1 Peter 2:2).*

Almost nothing compares to an infant's desire to eat. The baby will cry and cry until that mother's milk reaches his or her mouth. But when the baby begins to suck and they feel that milk, contentment comes (along with some interesting sighs and other sounds). The same is true with a new believer. The new birth has a great hunger to know God's Word. We must be there to 'feed' them His Word so that they can grow.

Life starts at the spiritual new birth (called "regeneration" in theological terms). Growth occurs when the believer acquires God's Word, just like when an infant receives nutrition.

A Mother's Tender Care

This need for God's Word will be constant throughout our lives. We need to eat to live, but something changes as we grow. At the early stage, the food and nutrition is in milk form and must be provided by the Mom. God designed this feeding to foster intimacy. When breast or even bottle feeding the baby, the Mom and baby can and do often look at each other.

As we think about spiritual new life, some basic elements are coming to the forefront: intimacy, bonding, love, the Word of God, care, and attention. There are obviously other necessities when caring for an infant but nothing is as important as these basic aspects of nurturing.

A great need

For years the church has had a healthy focus on bringing people into the kingdom of God, but many of these new babes have suffered post-birth trauma. They have not received the care they needed because they were never personally nurtured and cared for by other believers. They were not discipled. A baby cannot feed himself nor can a new believer. He needs to be fed and only later, after a period of growth, can he learn how to feed himself.

Although we may already know these basics, the problem is that we as the church have not been faithful to carry out what we know. So the body of Christ suffers terrible consequences. I regularly ask believers, "How many of you were personally cared for and taught as a new believer?" Few respond positively.

God's heart must be so broken due the lack of care we have for His precious children. Why isn't our heart equally broken? Why isn't the church repentant over its unwillingness to invest in raising up the next generation?

Lessons

- The new follower of Jesus Christ is likened to a little child, a baby, because he (or she) has similar needs that only can be provided by a caregiver.
- God wants us to care for new believers as a Mom gently and patiently cares for her little baby.
- God teaches new believers basic truths from God's Word during this early stage, bringing growth.
- The Lord wants the new child of God to sense His love and care through the personal attention of a disciple maker.

Memorize & Meditate

1 Peter 2:2

Assignment

➡ Were you discipled as a new believer? Explain what did or did not happen.

➡ How do you respond to new believers around you? Do you disciple them? Why or why not?

➡ If you were not discipled early on, what do you feel that you missed out on? If you were discipled, what things have you gained?

#16 The Young–Stage #2

The Teen

If the new believer requires intimate love and care, what does the young believer need?

The young person is known by the way he begins to take control of his own decisions. A transition takes place from when he is irresponsible and ignorant of what is right to that place where he understands and properly cares for himself and others. Young people are on the way to adulthood and certainly need to, at some point, learn how to care for themselves and others! Keeping God's overall goals in mind is extremely helpful to reduce the tension that otherwise can develop.

There are no easy markers for when this stage begins or ends. Many languages do not have a specialized word like 'teenager' to describe this transitional period. The original Greek describes this believer as "young", that is, not little and not mature.

The young believer's challenge

The young believer must learn how to use God's Word to stand strong against opposing influences and temptations. The Word of God is important, just as in the first stage, but here, the "youth" must learn how to face temptation. This is an integral part of being an overcomer.

The facts of life demonstrate this. When young people grow older, they must learn how to function in this world apart from their parents. This process is extremely slow for humans as compared to animals, but it eventually happens. While toddlers and preschooler are simply learning to feed themselves, those nearing adulthood need to learn to work to gain food so that he or she can eat.

Importance of God's Word

The older youth needs God's Word but can't regularly depend on others to feed them what they need. These believers are learning to approach God's Word to feed themselves. Additionally, they are learning how to use God's Word to protect themselves from the enemy that lurks about.

Note this strong wording from John which describes the young believer, "I have written to you, young men, because you are strong, and the word of God abides in you, and you have overcome the evil one" (1 John 2:13-14).

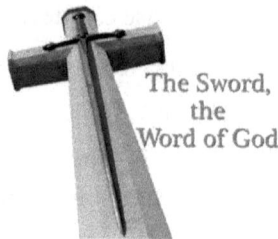

The Sword,
the
Word of God

This world is not as innocent and helpful as we would desire it to be. There is a very real enemy who seeks our demise. We should take comfort in the truth that Jesus Christ has already won the war, The young believer, however, needs to personally learn how to rely on God's grace when facing many different life situations.

Becoming strong

In the following verse, Peter boldly declares the power that derives from the truth of God.

For by these He has granted to us His precious and magnificent promises, in order that by them you might become partakers of the divine nature, having escaped the corruption that is in the world by lust (2 Peter 1:4).

The young like to think they are older than they are, demanding freedom without responsibility. They are unwary and ignorant of the challenges that face them. (Perhaps this helps them be eager for any challenge!)

Further steps of growth

The teenager resides between the two stages of "little child" and "adult". The desire for freedom to be an adult is good. They are catching on to the idea of where God is leading them. These "young men," however, still have childish patterns of thinking from when they were still a child. They still rely on others to feed them. As they mature, this needs to be resolved so that they can move into the "father" stage where they will care for others.

The wise lad establishes good spiritual disciplines and learns from others how to use God's Word to fight temptation. With a sharp eye, the young believer will notice that there is a battle within and a battle without. He will wonder why as a believer he still faces such a fight—even with those things which he despises. At the same time, he will sense the evil in the world that entices him to walk in its lustful and foolish ways.

Win!

God has won the battle and has fully equipped the young believer to fight and win! This will take a while to learn. There will be failures as well as successes. If someone disciples this believer, the training time will be shortened. The discipler can explain why spiritual life works the way that it does. He or she can help connect the dots so that lessons are more quickly learned. Otherwise, the new believer may have to fight many extra battles and perhaps suffer repeated defeats, leading to discouragement or perhaps worse.

We know that it is morally reprehensible to neglect a new baby, but care is also needed for the young believer, even though he may look mature due to his age or background. Oversight is very helpful during this stage and can greatly aid a believer when he or she faces trials and temptations.

Lessons

- Young believers face the challenge of learning how to use God's Word to live strong Christian lives.
- Spiritual battles will occur in our new lives because of our flesh and the enemy that uses the world to seek our harm.
- God promises that His Word can help us experience consistent victory.
- Spiritual oversight at this stage can greatly assist a confused young believer who may not understand why certain things happen in his or her spiritual life.

Memorize & Meditate

2 Peter 1:4

Assignment

➡ Do you have a strong spiritual discipline of feeding yourself in God's Word? Why or why not?

➡ Do you think the daily input of God's Word is important to a strong spiritual life? Why do you think this?

➡ Relate one defeat and victory. Reflect on each of them. Why did you fall? Why were you victorious?

➡ Are you mature enough to know what to say to someone battling with temptation?

#17 The Mature–Stage #3

John insightfully describes this third and last stage as "fathers." Although there might be some vagueness when one becomes a "young man", fatherhood is much more clear. Fathers have children.

Our modern world has destroyed the ease and pleasure of discussing life as God has organized it due to political correctness. If we can get beyond this and just think about our own families, we can acquire much understanding about God's spiritual goals for every believer. Why? Because each of us has had a father! Our fathers, though, were not necessarily good fathers. In fact, at the seminars I conduct, I find there are not many believers who have had good fathers. And even if they claim they had a good father, they do not have a clear understanding of what a good father is.

God's goals for us

There are three distinctive aspects about the mature believer stage:

(1) God wants to move all of us forward to this third and final stage of spiritual development.

(2) God wants each of us to lead others into a new spiritual life.

(3) The Lord desires that we responsibly care for those that gain spiritual life around us.

The design

First, the Lord desires and has so designed it that each of us is to move ahead to spiritual maturity. "Until we all attain to the unity of the faith, and of the knowledge of the Son of God, to a mature man, to the measure of the stature which belongs to the fullness of Christ" (Ephesians 4:13).

The "child" stage is a cute stage, but it is not the goal. Nor is the teen stage. They are still in training for what God has for them. The Apostle Paul defines this 'father' stage as a mature person (not pudgy, but spiritually mature) with the fullness of Christ. The marks of Jesus Christ should be clearly seen in our lives.

Although Paul uses fathers here, it is obvious that he, just like John, is not speaking only of the spiritual development of men, but women too. All believers, from every country and culture, are expected to grow to Christ's likeness in this age.

To grow, we must gain the vision of what God has for us. This requires faith. Our reasoning might go like this, "If the Lord wants us to grow, then it means that He has made it so that we can grow." These are faith-building truths (actually all truth, rightly learned, is faith-building). Once we know that all believers are meant to grow into Christ's image while on earth, then we must agree to the fact that God has made it so that we can grow—no matter what obstacles we might face. There are no valid reasons to elude this path to growth.

Thinking about others

Second, the Lord has designed it so that the mature bring forth new life. These are the facts of life, are they not? Our world has rejected life and wretchedly distorted this picture of procreation. But think about a person who grows up and finds a great person to marry. They then aspire to have children. These desires are built into us. When parents struggle to have children, it becomes very difficult for them.

Spiritually speaking, we must never forget our responsibility to share the gospel and lead others into a relationship with God through Jesus Christ. When we bring them into this new relationship, it becomes our responsibility to care for them. We are not all preachers or teachers of God's Word, but each person, is to take up the charge to seek the salvation and growth of those around them. (Sometimes, we ask another more appropriate person to care for a new believer.)

Strategically caring for others

Spiritual care

Lastly, we are to exercise spiritual care for those around us. We are to aid those we lead to the Lord but are also responsible to minister to those that God brings into our lives.

In this mobile world with people regularly changing jobs, Christians are moving around the world at a dizzying pace. Believers from other parts of the country or world might be located near us. We need to deliberately look out for opportunities to serve others. We don't do this out of pride, as this is God's means of caring for His sheep. He uses more mature believers to care for the spiritually younger lambs.

In many countries disease and disasters are creating uncounted orphans. It is humbling to see how so many churches and pastors have stepped in to adopt these children. Even though they themselves do not have sufficient food for their own families, they laboriously care for these neglected ones.

In a similar way, we need to do our job as the church to make sure everyone is being 'fathered,' that is, someone is spiritually caring for them. This is the Spirit reminding His people of God's charge to make disciples. **Discipleship directly reflects God's love and care for believers' development.** The development of small groups in many churches can greatly help in this process, but there will always be some that do not fit into our programs. Let's be alert to their needs.

What a shame if a father, who because he seeks to be comfortable, ignores the need of his children. That is wrong.

In a positive light, caring for others is God's great opportunity to transfer His love and wisdom to others. For men this will include their willingness to step up to church leadership positions in the church. This will also include special mentoring for couples, a sister with a sister, a man with another man. Pay attention to the needs of those around you. God just might want to use you to help them grow.

Lessons

- The 'fathers' are mature believers who have stepped beyond the struggles of the young believer and are able to focus his or her care on others.
- God's people can and should grow into full maturity in Christ.

- We are responsible to pass God's truth of life on to others and care for their spiritual development.

Memorize & Meditate

Ephesians 4:13

Assignment

➡ How long have you been a follower of Jesus? Are you a spiritual 'father'?

➡ Have you taken care of younger believers in Christ? How has that gone? How could it have been better?

➡ Is there anyone around you that you are now caring for?

#18 The Life Cycle

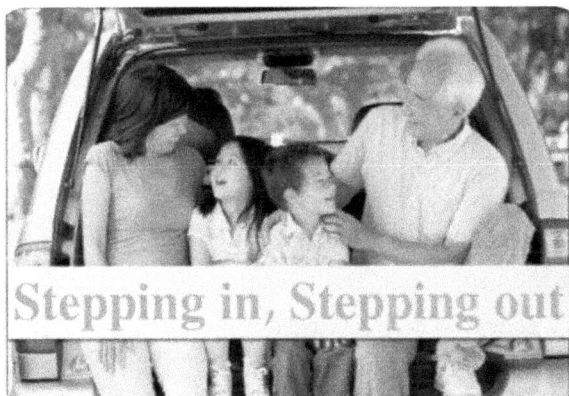

Stepping in, Stepping out

The cycle of life is not only true in the physical realm, but also in the spiritual world too. We are birthed into the world, go through struggles of growth and take on our share of bringing others into the world and caring for them. We then step out of this cycle to give others opportunity.

The full picture

This picture of the whole helps us develop clarity as to the limited time and special work God has for each of us in this life. We are not here indefinitely; time and opportunity are limited commodities. The earlier this mindset can be grasped, the more we can begin to understand God's purposes for bringing us into His sphere of grace.

Although our time on earth is short, it powerfully shapes the eternal. Our daily decisions are far more important than we normally would credit them. The way each of us conducts our lives greatly influences our lives in eternity. God makes sure of this.

Gaining a grasp of the whole

Understanding the full scope of spiritual growth gives us an edge on productive and fulfilled living. Here are three ways this happens:

- Responsiveness - We more easily awaken to the importance of our present state in life.
- Clarity - We gain a fairly clear picture of what already has or has not transpired through our lives.
- Focus - We sharpen our determination to reach maturity and fulfill His particular plan for our lives.

My father used to measure our increasing heights by marking the top of our heads on the doorframe with a pencil mark. I was always excited to see how much I had grown. The same is true with our spiritual lives. Believers are naturally curious about their personal spiritual growth. Some of it can be competitive, but there is a healthy anticipation of further growth leading to full maturity. This growth will continue to develop in this world, even after we have reached the mature stage.

The problem underlying much of the spiritual slackness among believers is that they have no goals and therefore become stagnant in their spiritual development. Instead of focusing on what God is presently set on doing in their lives, they become distracted with personal problems, ensnared in religious pride or are caught up in the world.

Two heart cries

After reading through the Bible books of Joshua and Judges, I became very aware of two deep cries in my heart.

(1) The Book of Joshua teaches my heart to hope for God's great work to be accomplished through my life. All is possible. Nothing can hold back the work of God in me or the church, local or worldwide.

(2) The Book of Judges humbles my heart. I grieve over how I have neglected my life responsibilities. I neglect to carry out what I could have very well done.

The full potential of victory sits right next to the awful shame of defeat. Each reminds the other of what could can happen. We are not victims, somehow caught in the bondage of non-growth. **Every moment of life, we stand on a threshold of opportunity.**

As we step through that doorway, we can evaluate where we are in our spiritual development. Our hearts are grateful to what God has done. But there are those other times that we have just ignored the principles of life—just as in Judges. What once excited us now has dropped from sight and heart.

Here are some life opportunities. What are yours?

- Are you living with a horrible spouse?
- Is your boss insensitive to your capabilities?
- Has someone just 'stolen' your girl?
- Are you getting grumpy over getting old?

If we observe problems in others around us or in our own lives, **we need to remember that we are sitting next to victory.** Did you ever notice that the power of the enemy never really matters in the Bible? This is simply because God is always greater, and so, **the Book of Joshua sits right next to Judges as our reminder.**

We cannot, of course, recapture the past, but we can step into the future brimming over with confidence that the Lord on high desires to maximize our service, no matter our past failures. God is prepared and ready to lead us on today.

The apostle admonishes us, "Therefore be careful how you walk, not as unwise men, but as wise, making the most of your time, because the days are evil. So then do not be foolish, but understand what the will of the Lord is" (Ephesians 5:15-17).

Time is one aspect of life that affects us all. Fortunately, by God's grace and a humble and seeking heart, even He can make up for lost time. Making wine takes time due to the fermentation process, but Jesus turned the water into wine in but a moment.

YOUR SPIRITUAL GROWTH CHART

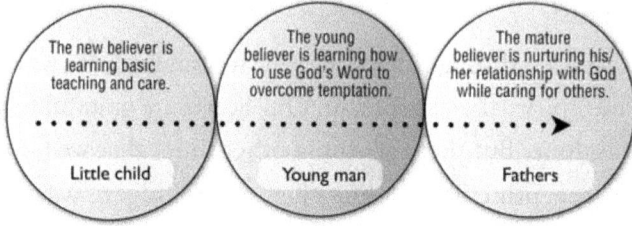

The new believer is learning basic teaching and care.

The young believer is learning how to use God's Word to overcome temptation.

The mature believer is nurturing his/her relationship with God while caring for others.

Little child

Young man

Fathers

How spiritually old are you?

Clarify where you are on the spiritual life chart. Note where you should be. Seek the Lord that He would move you to where you should be and seek to increasingly bear fruit for Him in your life.

Lessons

- Our limited time places an urgency on identifying where we are at on the spiritual growth chart and impels us to move forward.
- God wants to strategically work through our lives but an increasing growth and maturity are essential requirements.
- When we purpose to grow, then growth suddenly becomes easier and more exciting.

Memorize & Meditate

Ephesians 5:15-17

Assignment

➡ Indicate where you are on the spiritual life growth chart. Why do you suggest that spot?

➡ Do you sense the urgency of spiritual growth? In any case, talk with the Lord about this matter and ask Him to highlight your priorities in life at this point.

➡ Identify one task, routine, item, improvement, etc., that can help you focus on adopting the change that is needed for your personal growth. Write down how and when you will implement this. Talk to the Lord about it again (Proverbs 3:6).

(3) Practice the Life Core

Chapters 19-29

#19 The Purpose of Discipleship

By the time believers hear about these three stages they are often already very encouraged. When they understand the idea, it's like they've been given a new set of legs. Most of them have never considered thinking about the Christian life in stages. This includes most Christian teachers and preachers. Because of this, not many evaluative tools have been created to help us gauge where we are in our spiritual lives.

Things I don't know

Believers typically think spiritual life is unclear and confusing. Their summary goes something like this, "I'm saved and supposed to look towards heaven." They are rather confused about what the path of sanctification should look like.

My wife and I train parents on child rearing. We find the same problem there. With less and less experience at home due to the lack of large families or stay-at-home Moms, younger couples don't know how to care for their little ones.

One would think the basics, such as raising a child or breastfeeding, would be instinctive, but they aren't. There are things one must learn to properly breastfeed and raise good children. Instinct can be frustratingly unhelpful at times! This is the reason hospitals and midwife clinics have added such classes.

The same is true with Christ's teachings. Can we just sense God's presence and worship Him? Will believers just naturally grow? No, it does not work so innately as that, at least in our fallen world. Even the scriptures speak of many having problems rightly understanding spiritual matters such as: morality (Rom 2:14-15), God's presence and power (Rom 1:19-20), or the wrongness of selfishness. These things might not be clear. Meanwhile, our senses can easily overrule what vague knowledge we have.

Jesus instructed on discipleship

This is the reason Jesus told us to make disciples. We are to bring others to where they will learn about what Jesus said and what He has done. "Teaching them to observe all that I commanded you..." (Matthew 28:19).

I am glad to see more people teaching and writing about discipleship in recent years. However, I am dismayed that people think it largely has to do with a method rather than a path, focusing more on the content rather than the personal relationship. I appreciate the focus on how to individually train others. I also teach this because it is, in many cases, a forgotten art and relegated to expensive counseling sessions. We need to go beyond this, however. Our purpose is to teach so that others learn. This 'learning' is the real meaning behind discipleship.

Most of us feel much more comfortable with quantitative teaching, those things that can be tested on and measured. Western education has trained us this way. Spiritual matters, however, are not so easily tested and are therefore:

(1) More easily ignored

(2) Unclear (unless properly taught)

(3) Seemingly less relevant

Paul and others affirm the importance of the changes that take place when we rightly learn about Jesus, "And put on the new self, which in the likeness of God has been created in righteousness and holiness of the truth" (Ephesians 4:24).

Renewal in the mind (4:23) is important but must be followed with sufficient clarity and conviction to bring the needed transformation.

The power of truths in 1 John 2:12-14

I am excited at the teaching approach presented in 1 John 2:12-14. John at once makes it very simple to learn because we are all familiar with the family analogy, probably having grown up in a family or at least have seen others raised in one. God

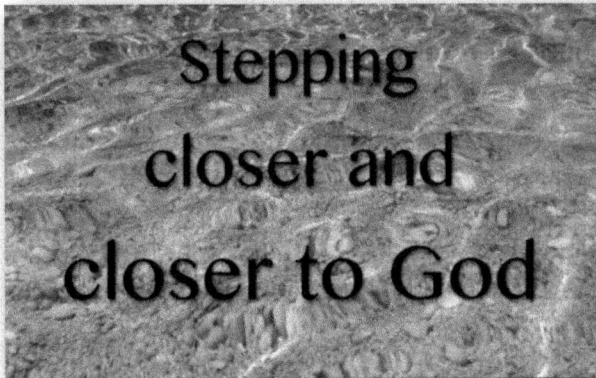

Stepping closer and closer to God

makes it easy to learn and grow.

More than this, though, John provides a complete system that helps us better learn the individual parts. These three stages were mentioned in the prior section, but this is just the beginning. Spiritual learning is much like wading deeper and deeper into the ocean. We may be hit by an unexpected wave or no longer be able to see the bottom, but God is beckoning us to come out further into the deeper waters. He wants us to trust Him with what He brings into our lives so that we may experience more of His glorious person and plans.

From a training perspective

In this section, *Practice the Life Core*, we will show how the whole system interrelates with the parts from an educational and training perspective. We have done this in a limited way on a personal level, but it is important to use this 'tool' or analysis to examine training in the church at large.

This approach helps us to come up with practical methods of training that can be implemented into our teaching that will further induce spiritual development in our training as opposed to merely knowledge-based learning. I am not sure that we can produce the quantitative measurements that teachers commonly look for, but we can certainly help you reach the goals God has for us when training others.

Ideally, a Christian teacher, whether in the church or school, desires to have each student spiritually grow to his or her fullness in Christ. If this is our goal, then we must cultivate the right atmosphere to foster eager learning. **Discipleship is a key concept that helps us move toward the goals God has for us.**

Lessons

- Discipleship describes the learning that happens when a more mature believer assists a younger one to learn essential things about Jesus that they may know how to live out strong, Christ-like lives.

- The challenge of Christian training, formal or informal, is to have the believer actually experience godly transformation.

- The lack of focus on measurable knowledge makes it difficult to evaluate quantitative learning.

- The life transformation that takes place when getting to know God through Christ is exciting; the teacher is able to see change in the student.

Memorize & Meditate

Ephesians 4:24

Assignment

➡ Give an example of when you learned about something but lacked the conviction to put it into action.

➡ Would you say that you are currently eager to grow spiritually? Why or why not?

➡ Have you ever discipled someone? Who? When?

#20 The Core of Life

Most of us live our lives totally oblivious to the inner workings of the earth. Perhaps, when there is an earthquake, we might wonder about what lies beneath our feet, but most of us go on living without ever giving it another thought.

Much of our Christian lives is the same. Christians are totally unaware of what goes on underneath the surface of their own Christian lives. Though the process of sanctification has been studied and written about extensively, there remains a subtle and hidden ignorance about what is most essential—spiritual life.

God's special work in us

Earlier in the book, we described the power of the life force working through the agent the Holy Spirit. Life is not just a general force but is personal, with a will, and purpose. When anyone consciously works along with the Spirit's purpose, then the power of that force is more readily felt and understood.

When believers are ignorant of the Spirit's intention, then they live in a life of ignorance which breeds various forms of confusion, leaving the believer living contrary to the Spirit!

There have been movements associated with Christianity that have identified certain streams of the Holy Spirit's work. They have been excited to latch onto what they call the 'fullness of the Spirit,' but unfortunately, more often than not, they too are ignorant of God's greater purpose in their lives.

The apostle purposely sandwiched 1 Corinthians 13, the chapter of love, in between the two chapters of 12 and 14 which address the gifts of the Holy Spirit. These gifts are certainly important or they would not have been mentioned repeatedly. Note, however, how the apostle interrupted that discussion to point us to something greater, "But earnestly desire the greater gifts. And I show you a still more excellent way" (1 Cor 12:31).

Focusing on the heart issues

The underlying purpose of the Holy Spirit is to make us more holy like Christ (Eph 3:17; 4:1-3). Gifts without holy living will be misused and abused.

The Holy Spirit's inner workings and purposes are what I have called the 'life core' because it is the heart of all that we do as believers. The Holy Spirit brings life but also illumines the believer. He not only gives us spiritual gifts but speaks through God's Word to stir us on to live out our lives in faith.

> *But when He, the Spirit of truth, comes, He will guide you into all the truth; for He will not speak on His own initiative, but whatever He hears, He will speak; and He will disclose to you what is to come (John 16:13).*

Understanding the Holy Spirit

Unfortunately, we can gain knowledge about the Holy Spirit without being impacted by Him. This is one basic problem of our knowledge-based education system. Our learning is not very well applied to our lives. The wind can blow without us being very aware of the breeze. The opposite is somewhat true, too. People can be moved by the Holy Spirit without understanding Him and His purpose. That is ignorance.

Living counter to the Holy Spirit's good and godly purposes is called 'disobedience.' Some know what the Holy Spirit wants them to do but do not carry out what He wants in the way that He desires it completed. King Saul is a sad and frustrating example of this hardness of heart. He squandered many good learning opportunities by forgetting his lesson.

Examining our attitudes helps us get a better picture of our inner persons. We are to give, but not begrudgingly (2 Corinthians 9:7). We are to serve others without complaint. How quickly do we accomplish that which God prioritizes?

Two general responses to God

It becomes easier and more joyful to align ourselves with God and His purposes when we fathom what amazing things He is doing through His Spirit in us.

Two models: The Holy Spirit's interaction with a believer

In the diagram above on the left, we see how ignorance and hardness of heart form a barrier between the believer and the Holy Spirit. On the right side, the barrier is taken down, allowing a flow of the Holy Spirit in the life of the believer (see appendix #3, The Flow). The believer, then, becomes more responsive to the Holy Spirit. This is the true meaning of "filled with the Spirit"–being wholly influenced by the person of the Spirit of God.

Clarity helps

Christian training should clearly identify the purposes of the Holy Spirit so that God's people can eagerly join in God's work. Unfortunately, many cannot clearly explain this work and so God's people as a whole are ignorant of what goes on beneath the surface of their Christian lives. Believers live out weak, anemic lives compared to what God desires for them.

The strength of the believer comes by connecting and affirming one's will with the work of the Holy Spirit (Romans 12:1-2).

Lessons

- Many believers are ignorant of the Holy Spirit's purpose in them and thus are oblivious or suspicious of His work.
- When the believer is unwilling to respond to the Holy Spirit's work, a spiritual hardness and unresponsiveness develops.
- When we clarify how God accomplishes His sanctifying purposes through the Holy Spirit, we receive a larger perspective of our spiritual lives, allowing us to understand and embrace Spirit-filled living.

Memorize & Meditate

John 16:13

Assignment

➡ Read John 16:5-15. Write down the things you observe about the Holy Spirit.

➡ Think of a recent time when you struggled with the Spirit's prompting—to do or not do something. What was the struggle about? How did you respond? What will you do next time? Why?

#21 Grasping the Vision

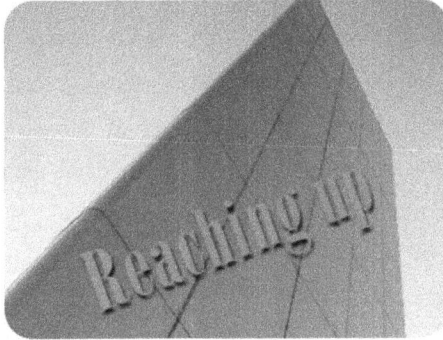

As teachers and trainers, we need to grasp the full implications of what God has for each believer, as well as for our own lives. Why? Because this is the faith that God would have us reach for, hold on to, and pass on to others.

Identifying our goals

There are many today speaking about goals, vision, and mission statements, but they actually have been embedded in the scriptures long before modern men and women thought of them. God acts according to a design because He is accomplishing His great plan. The work of creation is a marvelous plan, but so is His masterpiece—the Church of God and His grand redemption plan (see Colossians 1:15-20).

2 Chronicles 29 describes the amazing transformation that took place in Judah during Hezekiah's reforms. They penetrated much deeper than previous reforms of past kings because he had a hope for what could be.

Clarifying our goals with God's Word

That hope came from hearing God's Word. He envisioned what God wanted regarding the keeping of the Passover, and so he acted accordingly and invited all of Israel rather than just the southern kingdom of Judah. He did this because scripture highlighted the importance of having all the men of Israel participate. He braved the political controversy to carry out God's Word.

Our goals should be derived from what we find in scripture rather than what the culture tells us is important. The Bible teaches what God wants for our marriages, church life, personal relationships, and many other aspects of our lives. When the Word presents something different from what we experience or think, it challenges us with two questions,

(1) Do you believe God's goals for you should shape your personal goals?

(2) Do you believe God can help you reach these goals?

Goals and fruit

Just as every plant in our garden (even an unwanted weed!) is programmed to grow according to a hidden plan, so the Holy Spirit is unfolding His plan in each of us too. Our main hope for this book is to reveal the link between God's hidden plans and power in Jesus Christ with our own lives.

Of course, every person and ministry is unique, but there are commonalities. Think of the plants' roots, branches, leaves, and fruit. Each plant is unique and so is the context, and yet there are commonalities of function. The blackberry plant has similarities to the raspberry and yet remains very different. The difference goes much deeper than the colors and taste of the berries.

There are similar features on how Christian believers live out their godly lives, but there will also be unique calls and expressions of God's purpose in each follower of Christ. As they remain committed to growing and consecrating themselves to the Lord, our good Lord at the proper time reveals these things to them.[5] A plant does not bear fruit until sufficiently mature. If a plant is healthy and strong, it can bear much good fruit.

There is, then, a basic foundational task of equipping all of God's people but also a more specific training for individuals as their unique participation in God's kingdom work becomes clear. It's here where we will see the most significant growth and change take place as they begin to "bear fruit" (John 15:16). No one expects mature fruit on a young plant, nor should we early on focus on development of the fruit. Similarly, it is more important to focus our energies on identifying where a particular believer is in his or her growth, and then foster whatever development is needed. The fruit will come in time; God has made it this way.

And goes to bed at night and gets up by day, and the seed sprouts up and grows--how, he himself does not know. The soil produces crops by itself; first the blade, then the head, then the mature grain in the head (Mark 4:27-28).

Training keeps the larger goals in mind

This is the thrust of the life force that drives our new lives in Christ. He is bringing about His purposes and wants us to bear fruit in keeping with God's good and gracious purposes. (See appendix 1 for a helpful diagram.)

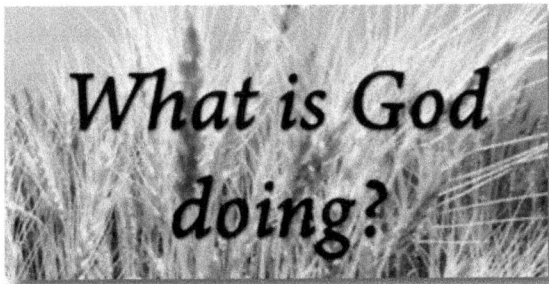

What is God doing?

---

[5] The timing issue sometimes becomes a testing place as it did for Abraham in Genesis 16.

If properly understood, training leads us toward these goals, not away from them. Some people, unfortunately, refrain from thinking about goals and standards.

Think of a little baby crawling around on the floor. The parents may begin to dream about the future of the child when he or she becomes an adult. They might say things like, "When she gets married...." "When he grows up...."

The infant, child, and teen stages of a person's life are all temporary because they are formational and preparatory. Good training begins by identifying where an individual is and then, step by step, implementing the necessary spiritual care and teaching. Without knowledge and experience, we merely mimic what we have experienced. That is good to a certain point, but we are still training in ignorance.

Training and parents

My wife and I teach parenting classes. When fielding questions (and there are many of them!), my wife wisely identifies what age the child is at before answering her questions. In the toddler years, a year or two can make a tremendous difference between what advice one would make.

When we understand what God has for us at each stage of our Christian lives, then the "how" of training becomes much clearer both to the trainer and trainee. We are not simply fulfilling some random church program, but training to help equip believers to fulfill specific goals, depending on their level of maturity.

As trainers, or more accurately mentors, both my wife and I are discovering God's will as we work alongside the Lord and seeking the best way to incorporate the needed training into the lives of the disciples. This is no different from how good parents train their own children.

God's purpose and power

The greatest thing about this process is the fact that Jesus Christ is that life force growing in us and leading us toward His goal of being like Him. This is not haphazard but a very specialized process. God is living in us to carry out His purposes!

We do not need to create this life nor force it to grow. If genuine, there will be that innate drive to grow and bear fruit. We are simply working along with what God is doing, much like a farmer tending to his garden. Remember, Jesus told Peter to "Feed my sheep." Peter did not need to give the sheep life but only to feed and tend them as a good shepherd.

The training starts with our lives and then it can more easily be transferred to others. Training, then, is simply teaching others what God already has been doing in our own lives.

Lessons

- Spiritual vision is born from scriptural truths that shape our expectations and focus.
- Goals need to be specific for each stage of spiritual development.
- We are not creatively devising goals to guide growth but carefully observing what God has said in the scriptures and connecting that to our lives.
- God has special plans for each believer to bear God's love and light in this dark world. This is his or her fruit (also called "good works").

Memorize & Meditate

Mark 4:27-28

Assignment

➡ What are God's goals for you at this point in your life? Try to identify at least three.

➡ How do you respond to making and setting goals? Are you excited or frustrated by the process? Explain why.

➡ What is the long term goal God has for some garden plants or crops? What does that mean in the spiritual context of your life?

➡ Remind yourself of the process to reach the goal mentioned above, then think of a few believers around you. Pray for each that God would help them to grow. If God speaks to you in a specific way to help them, follow up.

#22 Our Limitations

The long term goal of the believer is to grow into Christ's likeness, but this needs to be more specifically defined. The more clearly we envision what God wants for our lives, the easier it is to obtain this goal.

Working with our limitations

As a trainer, a school, a parent, etc., we will quickly discover that God's goals for those we are working with go far beyond what we can do. That is something we need to recognize and accept.

First, accept that our training with a certain individual will be subjected to time limitations, perhaps a month, a year, five years, etc. Similarly, our time with them will also vary. We might teach a class for an hour a week or personally meet several times each week one-on-one with someone.

Second, it is important to think of ourselves as God's assistants. God is accomplishing His own purposes in each individual. He works through us to help Him work out His purposes in others. Jesus powerfully rebuked both those who saw themselves better than others as well as those who work apart from God's purposes.

But do not be called Rabbi; for One is your Teacher, and you are all brothers....And do not be called leaders; for One is your Leader, that is, Christ (Matthew 23:8,10).

Jesus does not mean that we should not have teachers or call certain individuals as a teacher (i.e., Rabbi, see James 3:1), but He was addressing our attitudes about our degrees, position, and research. We have to realize that we are working along with God to facilitate a person's spiritual development. Though significant, we are not the key. The image of nurturing physical life helps us here. We do not cause a person to grow but only make it easy to grow.

LONGTERM GOALS
TIME
PURPOSE
SHORT TERM GOALS

Rightly discerning our part

When we step back into our school or church positions, we can see that we might have the gift of leadership or teaching given from the Holy Spirit (Romans 12:7-8). That same Spirit uses what He imparts into us to further the growth of others. Our training period might seem frustratingly short, but have faith. Trust God for the shaping that takes place in that period of time. Anticipate how you can best foster that growth which God wants to bring into the life of the student or disciple during that time.

Also remember this is God's "greater work." Labor in confidence that the Lord has a complete work in mind for each individual and our contribution is small though significant.

Discovering our limitations

After examining what the long term goals are, and they will be the same for each believer, we need to discern what specific stage of growth the person we are working with is in. Considering our time, situation, resources, gifts, and God's purposes. What is God trying to accomplish through this time? Let's look at each aspect.

Time: Determine how much time we might have with the trainee. For example, we might have thirteen hours of class time. Plan what can be done in each hour and be sure to use take-home assignments.

Situation: Is the learning situation an adult Sunday School class, a college class, mentoring time, or some other venue? Our situation often directs us to what we need to discuss, and hopefully, we can see how this fits into the larger goal. For example, the pastor might want you to use an eight-week discipleship booklet when meeting up with a certain believer, or the seminary wants you to fulfill their objectives for a class.

Resources: Our resources largely shape what we can do. One ministry context may use prescribed books while another has no printed materials whatsoever. One may have computers while another doesn't even have sufficient funds to travel to class. Be alert to these needs. Limited resources often challenge effective training, but perhaps God is training you through the difficult circumstances to further encourage others with how God can work, despite the limitations.

Gifts: Hopefully what we do largely lines up with how God has spiritually gifted us. This is important because we have increased faith to carry out our service along the lines of our spiritual gifts. Do remember, though, our giftings might not be able to be worked out as we would want in a given situation. This requires patience and the seeking of God's wisdom.

God's purposes: This, perhaps, is the most important aspect of all. God is not restrained by our circumstances, even when we might have limited gifts or resources. Prayer, faith, and careful deliberation of what God is desiring to do remain important during these times.

Understanding our roles

Some people feel rather comfortable and ready while others are confused and helpless. The more we grab a hold of what God wants to do, the more we see how very little we can contribute. No matter how small that task might be, God still greatly values your service. It is never to be despised.

Think of the man standing with a hose watering his desperately needy plants. He is not bringing life or growth, but through his service, God is able to accomplish His greater works. Small service? Yes. Great contribution? Yes!

I planted, Apollos watered, but God was causing the growth. So then neither the one who plants nor the one who waters is anything but God who causes the growth (1 Cor 3:6-7).

So, although we need to be aware of our numerous limitations, we do not allow them to lessen God's standards or cause us to despise our contributions. Nor do we think more highly of ourselves than is proper. The lack of faith (doubt) as well as pride are destroyers of God's wonderful work that He desires to do through us in the lives of others.

Strengthening our faith to train

When examining God's goals (these might be significantly different from your pastor's or department head's goals), we wonder how we can ever fulfill these goals in the allotted limitations, time, or otherwise. We need a miracle.

Each time I conduct an overseas bilingual three-day training seminar for Christian leaders, I face this dilemma. Time is limited. Language is a barrier. It may be very hot. I remember once in India we had a noisy idol parade outside the teaching site. Loud firecrackers were competing with our messages.

It is essential that as teachers we conduct ourselves in faith. Do not let discouragement rule, for then we will take our eyes off God's greater purposes. Give God room to make his Name great through the training times. He can accomplish more in one minute than we can in one hour. Our faith is buoyed by understanding God's whole purpose of building up His people. "And I also say to you that you are Peter, and upon this rock I will build My church; and the gates of Hades shall not overpower it" (Matthew 16:18).

Peter had much authority given to Him, but still Jesus insisted that it was He that built His church and nothing would be able to frustrate His plans.

Living God-dependent lives

If our goals are properly formed in light of God's great purposes, we will always see that we only foster life rather than create it. We are not the Teacher, Christ is. As under-teachers and trainers, we need to focus on our part. As we do this, God seeks to fill us with His Spirit to be able to accomplish all that God wants in our limited time and circumstances!

Whether we teach a sermon series, a Sunday School class, small group, etc., we live in light of God's greater purposes and therefore humbly seek His empowering that we may properly carry out His wonderful works. (Although I focus on teaching, this is true for anyway that God works through us.)

Remember Christ's rebuke. If we think we have mastered these things, then we are part of the problem rather than the solution. God causes the genuine growth and thus brings our students from one stage of development to another.

Christ is the Master Teacher. It is His Spirit who works in both the teacher/trainers as well as in each student/disciple. He looks for mediators by which He can effectively pass on His truth. Let's properly perceive our crucial task of holding out the water of life to these precious students. Perhaps we might end up praying more!

Lessons

- Longterm goals help us better appreciate our small but significant place in teaching.

- Because we are limited in time and otherwise, we need to humbly seek God for wisdom on how to best use our resources to accelerate the growth of the believer.

- We must teach and mentor in faith so that God would take the little we have and multiply it to accomplish His greater good.

- The best teacher sets His heart on working by the Lord's side as His faithful assistant.

Memorize & Meditate

1 Corinthians 3:6-7

Matthew 23:8,10

Assignment

➡ Name the most significant lesson you've learned from this chapter. Pray over it.

➡ Do you tend to possess high goals and become frustrated, or have low goals and be ineffective? Please explain.

➡ How can this lesson help high or low achievers improve their perspectives of teaching?

➡ Meditate on 1 Corinthians 3:5-10 and summarize what is the best approach to teaching and training others.

#23 The Parts of the Whole

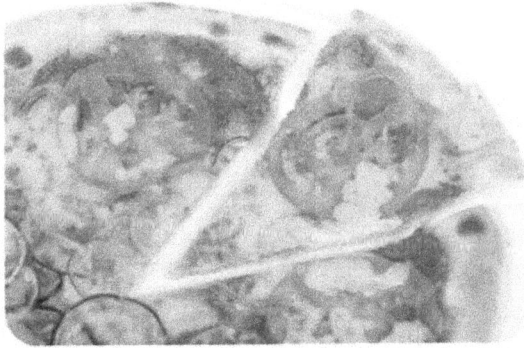

One significant problem with training is not being able to fully understand how God's overall goals are to be accomplished. John's breakdown of the believer's spiritual journey in 1 John 2:12-14, however, provides just what we need to help us understand growth at any particular level.

Understanding marks of growth

The analogy of life, articulating the source, power, design, and drive of life are very helpful, but it doesn't help us reach measurable goals. We use measurable goals to easily present and challenge others to adopt and pursue. John not only distinguishes one level from another, but he also identifies the chief areas of growth that are to occur at particular levels. These become our major goals.

Specific spiritual goals are similar to signs of growth in a child. A toddler's first steps or the speaking in complete sentences are common marks of physical development. These marks are indirect goals as they are not ones that we can directly affect (though we try!). The parents' job is to provide the general care and an environment conducive to growth.

One or two of my children were slow to start speaking. As parents we wondered if something was wrong. Fortunately, there was nothing wrong. We had to learn that each child develops at a different pace. Although we cannot do much to speed up this development, these marks of growth are very significant; they tell us all is well.

In today's world with its stock pile of research, medical staff can often tell what is wrong if a child is not developing properly. Perhaps a child is lacking a certain nutrient for proper development. There are several options: The chemical could be supplemented, or further created by stimulating the right body organ, or perhaps surgery is needed. All the solutions, however, must work within the context and rules governing the body if they are to be successful.

Spiritual goals

This is the same situation with our spiritual needs. We do not make the system, but rather work along with it. We place our confidence in the spiritual system that God created. It works. Spiritual growth occurs, and the scriptures have provided the growth marks to help gauge our growth. As God's appointed teachers and trainers, we encourage this general growth pattern.

The marks of growth become our goals not because we make people grow, but because it forces us to be aware of what God is doing in people at different stages. To encourage and foster positive growth we supplement what is needed. Notice Paul's three goals for his teaching, "But the goal of our instruction is love from a pure heart and a good conscience and a sincere faith" (1 Timothy 1:5).

John has identified various things that need to happen at each stage. We can further complement these thoughts by using the physical development analogy. I personally have found that John's analogy provides easily transferable concepts as well as identifies practical steps of implementation. They are simple and yet profound.

As an instructor I have dug deeply at each well but never have yet found the time to plumb the full depth of each level's learning. Like mining, one can always dig a little deeper.

Great training

The key to great training rests in how we connect these two greater aspects:

(1) The clarity by which we relate all the parts of growth to God's overall purpose of spiritual development, and

(2) The strategic spiritual care and instruction needed at any given moment for an individual.

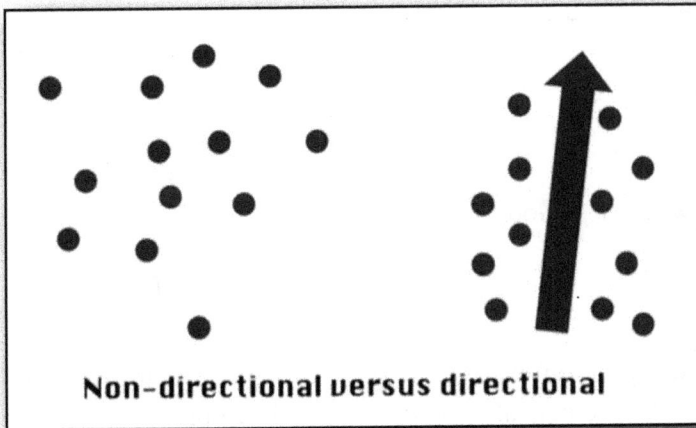

Non-directional versus directional

Believers face great problems when they do not receive proper training. The difficulties worsen when we see stagnant believers in the congregation drifting away from the Lord. In many places, we see these problems in the church getting worse. I believe it is largely because these two crucial steps are typically missing from the church, and therefore, believers are not receiving proper care.

Lessons

- The holistic picture of what God is doing helps us keep everything in perspective.
- The biggest problems in training occur due to a separation of the parts from the whole, short term goals from long term goals (i.e., God's goals).

Memorize & Meditate

1 Timothy 1:5

Assignment

➡ List the major responsibilities in your life, school, work, etc.

➡ How does God want you to grow spiritually and serve Him?

➡ What is God's long term goal for your life here on earth

➡ Have you ever connected your spiritual life with God's longterm goal for your spiritual development?

#24 Training with a Purpose

Before discussing what actually needs to happen at each stage of growth from a training perspective, let us see how the whole shapes our understanding of the individual parts.

Our goal to make disciples

In this case, let us think of the goal to make disciples. Perhaps we have personally discipled three individuals. (Discipleship is a specialized form of training.) Assuming they are now grown, like most parents we are proud of their growth, and yet we may be a bit concerned with a few areas of their lives (also like parents!).

During their training we need to be careful about what we are teaching them. A significant goal for them is that, like ourselves, they should feel compelled to disciple others. We can't be content on whether we have obeyed this command but whether those we have trained others to have this same vision to make disciples.

Can those we have trained go and disciple others? Do they know how? Do they care? Are they themselves training so that our disciples' disciples will train? Paul was doing this.

And the things which you have heard from me in the presence of many witnesses, these entrust to faithful men, who will be able to teach others also (2 Timothy 2:2).

This 2 Timothy passage well describes the discipleship process. Paul trains Timothy. Timothy, in turn, trains others so that they themselves will train others.

As much as I do not like role playing, I find it sometimes necessary to use to help the leaders I am training to sense what is really expected of them. We need to look far ahead to the end goal which in turn gives light on how we should teach.

Another goal is to have a great marriage

Many young people are now putting marriage off or are rejecting it altogether. I think it is largely because they are no longer convinced marriage is great. Inadvertently, they become promiscuous. Christian parents share their responsibility for their children's attitudes. Without knowing it, they are discipling. They may have been content to stay together, but this is a very low goal for marriage. The couple needs to have a marriage and family that their children would also aspire to have including harmony, interaction, mutual delight, practical love, and life-changing devotion.

Any couple that stays together for the kids is not thinking ahead. If the married couple is merely putting up with each other until the children are gone, they show their children why they should despise marriage and not get married.

A goal to train Christian students

What about our Christian schools and educational institutions? Are they considering what God wants as a whole? More than often, the short term goals, greatly influenced by our modern educational system and the expectations of the government, end up shaping curriculum and methodology more than what God says He is doing.

Christians try to counter this pressure by holding chapels where spiritual life messages are shared. This is commendable, but is it enough? In most cases, we will find that it is not. Christians need to be personally challenged at a level appropriate to their spiritual growth rather than just satisfy some requirement of attending some chapel service.

Certainly God can use these times to reach responsive students, but those that are bitter will only get more hardened.

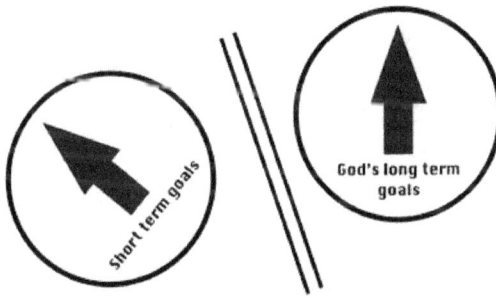

A Major Disconnect

A crisis in my life

Let me close with an example. After graduating from a solid Bible school, finishing several years of language learning, and completing an internship in a good church, I finally saw my dreams coming true. I was an overseas missionary and became part of a great team of nationals along with a few other missionaries to start a church! People started coming to know the Lord. What a wonderful first baptismal service was held there in a parking lot of a new residential area in southern Taiwan.

It was after this I experienced one of those life-shaking realizations. I did not know what to do with these new believers other than have them attend services and join us in some "Christian" activities. It is not that I did not take mission courses during Bible School. I even took a seminary class on church planting. I had a class on discipleship too. But something was amiss.

How could that which is so essential to Christian leadership be so lacking from my training? That was many years ago now, but I often think about that shocking realization.

A crisis in the church

Somehow I was not taught how the believer grows and how to assist them at each stage of development. The process of building disciples was absent from my training.

Since then I have had much time to assess my training and that of those around me. I found that I never gained an overall grasp of what God is doing. The theology classes on sanctification never were applied to the area of discipleship. Scriptures that were preached on somehow never crossed over and created an understanding of how they were related to the whole spiritual life growth process.

Having traveled and taught in many countries and churches, I see that this problem is not limited to geography, denomination, or educational institutions. Few believers and churches have a vision for building up their people through discipleship training. Even the churches that are on fire and have a great zeal and devotion rarely have discipleship training, largely due to not having connected the parts of training to the whole.

Would it be a proper assessment that after two thousand years, the church still has not understood and implemented the basics of discipleship? Why is it that the most elementary things have been neglected?

In my opinion, one of the biggest hindrances to the building up of a movement of godly people devoted to God and rightly training others is the lack of an overall picture of Christian life. Christians have not clearly thought through the fact that each believer is at a different place in his or her spiritual life process and needs specific instruction to get him or her on to the next step or stage of development.

The lack of a strong God-given goal allows many other smaller and inadequate goals to satisfy our training pursuits. When our overarching goal is set in place by thinking through John's life analogy, however, then John's growing analogy provides just what we need to fix and maintain short term training.

Lessons

- Short term goals must be shaped and connected to the larger spiritual life goal that the Lord has for each believer.
- It is urgent that we train others to have this vision to also train others.
- The full vision of Christian life and experience is not adequately passed on because few practically relate the whole purpose of God with the short term goals John provides for us.

Memorize & Meditate

2 Timothy 2:2

Assignment

➡ Have you ever been trained to disciple others? Are you in fact doing it?

➡ If so, what level of believer were you trained to work with? Explain how.

➡ If married (if not, think about your parents), is your marriage one that you would desire for your children?

#25 Taking Careful Aim

Aiming Carefully

As teachers and mentors, half of our problem is knowing what to teach, the other half is getting our students motivated to learn. In every case, though, limited time will shape our challenge of effectively training others.

God's life plan for our spiritual growth is always actively taking place just below the surface. We can trust Him to effectively carry out His part. But is it powerful enough to counter the world's increasingly diabolical forces? Sure it is. The problem resides with the church not properly carrying out its given task.

Getting perspective

We need to rethink the way we train our people, both in formal educational settings such as seminary and church, as well as in informal training situations such as at home or one-on-one. Only when we get more strategically focused will we be able to succeed. Our past methods are not effectively developing God's peoples and leaders. The living waters are not abundantly flowing. So many leaders complain that they do not have a sufficient number of leaders, while those that do, often fuss about the problems of those leaders.

Many teachers start off with great expectancy but then give up. The problem is not whether our students can be victorious, though. John says that His people are overcomers, even as young believers! Can you see this faith that energizes and directs the teacher and the student? But in many cases, the students do not possess this faith. In these situations, the teacher's faith has to be enough for both himself and the student.

Think about a class of new students. What is their level of growth in their character, knowledge, and skills? The teacher needs to take the goals of the course and break it down into teachable components–usually into single class periods.

Because time with students is so limited, we need to carefully choose our topics and course materials. What can we assume is true of the students? How far have they progressed? Where should they be by the end of the course? Or in a larger context, where should the members be after five years in the church or at what level should the students be at graduation?

Isn't it good to learn about the Bible?

We assume a good knowledge of the Bible is enough for the students going into full-time ministry. No doubt that is true. So the teachers get busy shaping their courses, such as *An Introduction to the Old Testament* and *An Introduction to the New Testament*. As time permits, specific courses like the *Gospel of John,* etc., are added.

This is good, but is it best? When we look at the general needs of the student, i.e., the need for Bible knowledge, it makes great sense. I met one Indian evangelist who was beat up because he couldn't explain why the Bible doesn't explain where the great number of people came from in the early chapters of Genesis.

I know there are pastoral majors, or mission, youth or counselor tracks in our Bible schools, but they are addressing what we will be doing rather than who we are. *The Life Core* challenges this perspective because it requires a deeper examination of what a student needs to learn and how he learns it. Only as we identify how God trains can we effectively coordinate our own methods with His.

Our point is not to be critical of the training around us. Many have been greatly aided by the courses taken, including me. We urgently need, however, to sharpen our vision. Our goals are generally right, but they are detached from God's principal means and purposes of training.

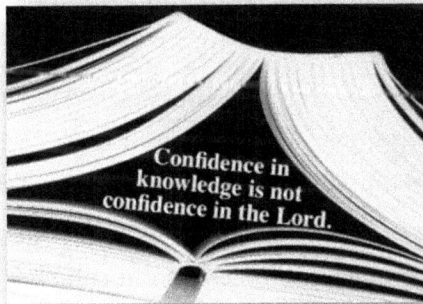

Confidence in knowledge is not confidence in the Lord.

Fine tuning of the mind

While continuing to use the example of basic Bible classes, we need larger goals than acquiring Bible knowledge alone. Here are a few considerations.

- We can get puffed up on our knowledge of God's Word.
- We wrongly learn God's Word so that it does not help us in our spiritual lives (e.g., Pharisees).
- We can even learn God's Word in a way that undermines our faith (e.g., the Sadducees who did not believe in a resurrection).
- We must learn God's Word in such a way that we can better hear God speaking to our hearts.

- We need to learn God's Word to know how it applies to the daily challenges we face.
- We learn that God increases faith as we acquire more knowledge of God's Word (not necessarily true!).
- We must have a prepared heart to rightly learn God's Word.

The list could go on, but these have been mentioned to help us realize that a great challenge is before both the teacher and the student. Jesus states this so clearly.

> *...You will be ever hearing but never understanding; you will be ever seeing but never perceiving. For this people's heart has become calloused; they hardly hear with their ears, and they have closed their eyes. Otherwise they might see with their eyes, hear with their ears, understand with their hearts and turn, and I would heal them (Matthew 13:14-15–NIV).*

We should not assume that Bible knowledge alone will help us when many times it does the opposite. The best of milk can go sour. Unless our students 'understand with their hearts and turn' to the Lord, there will be no genuine healing or learning.

Is not this one main problem in our churches? The Word is not preached to transform but to entertain. People have lost confidence that God's Word can change or should produce actual change in their lives. The typical time of worship is not leading God's people into holy living. Is it because they have not entered God's presence or heard God's Word? Much more has to go on under the surface to properly prepare the hearts of God's people.

Lessons

- Spiritual training must be integrated into all of our training. The importance of spiritual goals must outweigh educational ones.
- In many cases teachers have mistakenly assumed that knowledge is the primary need of students.

- Our training must be reevaluated in light of God's training process, otherwise our special opportunities of instruction will be wasted.

Memorize & Meditate

Matthew 13:14-15

Assignment

➡ Have you taken any Bible related classes (including Sunday School)? What has made the best classes great? What made the bad ones terrible?

➡ Did you feel that your education/training prepared you for service? Explain how.

➡ What could have been improved?

#26 Bridging the Gap

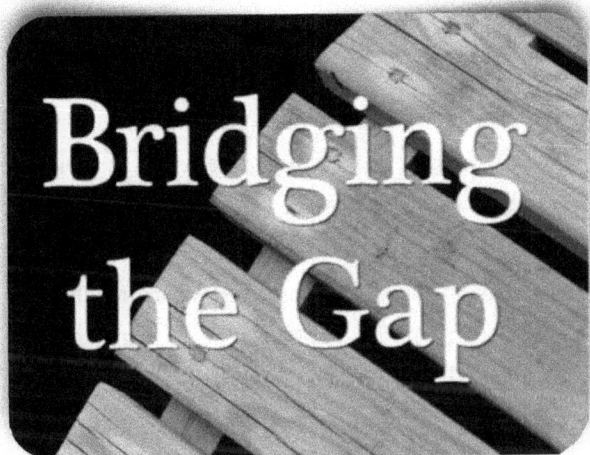

Western education puts its trust in knowledge. Christians must refute this approach to education and especially theological education. We are compelled by a greater goal: releasing the power of God's Word in people's lives.

The disconcerting disconnect

The disconnect between theological training and effective ministry remains huge. Those graduating are hardly ready for what is ahead of them. The world's solution to this problem is to require more education. Master and doctorate degrees are now commonplace, and the old assumption that knowledge itself is all that is needed has not changed.

Of course, much can be said for the effort to gain these degrees. The self-discipline itself is a great reward, but we must begin to draw back the curtain and look behind the scenes. Do we dare ask if our students are ready for life and ministry? In most cases they are not.

Our educational approach assumes that with the right knowledge, man will proceed to do great things. This is an offshoot of humanism. Knowledge is part of the equation but is not the whole. There are more important elements, including the spiritual shaping, that must take place in our Christian lives.

Confidence in knowledge often distances us from people rather than connects us together. Spiritual maturity is wrongly equated with theological training, but it is far from it. When there is an emphasis on knowledge, then there is little time to develop the heart and ministerial skills to effectively live godly lives and effectively serve. For instance, we learn about the field of higher criticism but have little time to learn how to allow God to teach us through the Word so we can teach others.

We are glad to hear about exceptions, but as a whole our upcoming church leaders are being improperly trained at a great financial outlay. These things no doubt contribute to half of all seminarians leaving the ministry after five years.[6]

Why the failure?

Why is there all this confusion and failure? Is it because the Word of God has failed? Or is it possible that the Word of God has not penetrated our hearts? Or have we not received the training needed to properly minister in the churches?

The Apostle Paul concludes the reason for little faith is that the Word of God has not reached the hearer's ears. In the parable of the Sower, however, Jesus takes this thought deeper. He says that God's people are not properly learning because their hearts are not prepared to receive it.

---

6 Pastor for Life by Ivan Charles Blake. Statistics vary widely but surely there are problems in the system. www.ministrymagazine.org/archive/2010/07-august/pastor-for-life Perhaps the rate is not so high but still greatly concerns us.

What if we change our focus around to prepare the hearts of these students so that they can properly acquire God's Word? They need to learn how to gain faith in God's Word rather than simply reading it as an assignment or only studying what other people say about the Bible.

Lack of faith

During my studies, one Old Testament professor told my class, "This might be the only time you read the Old Testament in your life." Carefully consider what he erroneously taught!

- The Old Testament is not important.
- The Old Testament is not be relevant to your lives.
- You will not want to read the Old Testament anymore after reading it this once.

He perhaps was unintentionally making a statement about his personal beliefs. Of course, the above bulleted points are not accurate but simply a view of scripture that lacks faith. While he never said it directly, he seemed to believe, "It's not relevant to my life, and I don't believe that you will think the Old Testament is relevant to your lives either." This was the message that was being clearly communicated.

As students begin plodding through their Old Testament readings, they will increasingly dread the Old Testament. There is no chance for their faith to grow in such a scenario. The professor knows, however, this class is 'important' because all students must take the class to graduate.

Some professors may not even think the Old Testament is reliable (unlike how the Old Testament or Jesus presents it). They teach it like a critic, further undermining the faith of their students. Other professors believe it to be reliable, like the one I referred to, but did not believe it was relevant to our lives and ministries.

These same sorts of things happen again and again whenever a preacher merely preaches a sermon. Without first being refashioned by the Word of truth, the preacher lacks the radiant faith needed to speak forth its relevance.

An abounding faith

Jesus taught the Old Testament in a completely different way. He lived a godly life from only the Old Testament. He quoted from the Old Testament when He was tempted, and His faith in God's Word protected Him. Jesus understood what God the Father had for His life through the Old Testament.

> *And after He had fasted forty days and forty nights, He then became hungry. And the tempter came and said to Him, "If You are the Son of God, command that these stones become bread." But He answered and said, "It is written, 'Man shall not live on bread alone, but on every word that proceeds out of the mouth of God (Matthew 4:2-4).*

Importance of reevaluating our methods

The importance of reexamining our learning process and content has never been more urgent. The teacher must go beyond delivering content and pay close attention to the faith needed to build up the faith of the students in that particular area. This faith is directly related to obtaining the goals God has for us.

There is a reason why God's people around the world have stopped growing. God's people are being trained to be content with knowledge rather than seeing God accomplish His goals.

"It is written..."

If we are going to have success tapping into God's life purposes and power, we must refute the claim that knowledge can by itself solve the problem. We need God's Word to actively work in our lives.

Most students come out of Bible school or seminary relying on their knowledge rather than God. Fortunately, God can and does work through our systems and does some good through them, but what would happen if we expected students to be changed to act and minister like Jesus? Our Lord in heaven is waiting for us to get our training right for the sake of His sheep and the honor of His Name.

- What if our students could learn how to step smoothly directly from school into ministry? (What would it take in terms of knowledge, skills, devotion, character, etc.?)

- Or in a church context, what would happen if God's people really did grow into full maturity? (What would need to happen in a church to get members there?)

We are definitely expecting far too little of our students and God's Word because we the teachers have so little faith. Jesus, however, had great faith in God's Word, even the Old Testament. "It is written...." The point is, God has spoken and His Word still remains powerful today.

Lessons

- The trust in knowledge confuses our goals of training, both in formal and informal training.

- A teacher's faith influences a student's learning and faith, for both good and bad.

- Only by recommitting ourselves to believe God's Word like Jesus will our teaching become relevant, dynamic, healing and helpful.

Memorize & Meditate

Matthew 4:4

Assignment

➡ Take any two Bible related classes, recent or in the past, and state what the objectives of the classes were. (Think of seminary, Sunday School, etc.)

➡ What kind of faith did the teachers possess regarding this topic? How do you know?

➡ How did these classes help or hurt you?

#27 Training New Believers

Caring for the little ones

In the past chapters we have identified what we believe to be the major flaws of leadership training that have resulted in weak, ungodly, and unequipped leaders and churches.

Although we cannot here give a full explanation of what needs to happen at each stage of Christian development, we will hopefully present sufficient understanding of what should be taking place. This will be introduced from the perspective of the instructor, pastor, or discipler, to help them think of how they, at a minimum, need to prepare God's people.

Instructing new believers

The power of John's presentation displays itself in the way John introduces each stage of spiritual development. John categorizes believers into three groups (note it is not by denomination!):

little children, young men, and fathers. This section will focus on new believers, the little children.

> *I am writing to you, little children, because your sins are forgiven you for His name's sake.... I have written to you, children, because you know the Father (1 John 2:12-14).*

In a past lesson, we briefly discussed how a baby, a picture of the new believer, requires special care and feeding. That is a cue for us as teachers and trainers. From John's words, we can clearly identify what God's major goals are for this stage of Christian development. At the same time we can understand how we need to train new believers. **God's goals for believers and our training must be interrelated.**

Small attempts

Somehow this specific need for making disciples (Matthew 28:20) has not been effectively undertaken. Few pastors believe making disciples is important, though they would certainly never say that. Their actions, or lack thereof, support my conclusions. Although thankful for the persistent calls to believe upon Christ, our neglect on caring for new believers is embarrassing. We would be shocked if we saw a woman give birth to her child and just walk away, thinking her job was done. Some evangelists, such as Billy Graham, in his later years have worked a bit more on follow-up, but the tradition of preaching with very little follow up training reveals one huge flaw that produces weak believers.

No matter what our church history or tradition has handed down to us, the church is called by God to lavish love on the new believer and provide personal spiritual care. At the same time, especially in the beginning stages, the church needs to be trained to provide that care. The pastor/evangelist/teacher is there to equip the church to carry out her basic functions of making disciples.

The vision of training

Our other books on discipleship provide extensive training in these areas, but it is important that we get a glimpse of how this works out in training settings.

First, as trainers we must extend the vision that it is the responsibility for more mature believers to nurture and provide for the basic care of new believers. A two-year believer, properly trained up, should be capable of training another new believer.

Second, we will define what this basic care looks like. This includes being a friend, taking special interest in their life problems, teaching them basic truths in God's Word, and sharing about how to handle problems they are facing. More difficult problems can be passed to the pastor.

Third, we need to show how new believer training fits into the whole picture of spiritual development and training. This perspective helps the trainer pass the vision of what is happening to the new believers and will be used to train other new believers in the future.

Fourth, identify what new believers are to learn and master at that first stage of Christian growth. This will include finding or developing training materials (that perhaps take seven to ten weeks to complete) that they can use to guide their times with new believers.[7]

John actually has quite a lot to say about this whole process at each level. There are other scriptures we can learn from as well. We can quickly gain a collection of discipleship tools for these new believers that will, in turn, be what they can use to train other new believers.

---

[7] In our *Initiating Spiritual Growth in the Church* seminar (Discipleship #3), trainers learn how to develop their own curriculum to fit their own needs and circumstances.

A greater perspective

God works in both the discipler and the disciple simultaneously. Think of the mother and the infant. God is pleased to see the mother feed the child that He has brought into the world. The mother is blessed to see how God uses her as she feeds her child (though there are struggles too!). Likewise, the hunger pangs of the new children of God reminds the more mature of their duty to nurture them. As God's people offer personal care and advice (discipling) to these new believers, they too will be enriched, seeing how God works through their small but essential contribution to the new believer.

The spiritual trainer must not be satisfied with training the new believers that have come under his or her care. They must envision them to train others, though this will take extended contact and commitment. Disciples largely learn through our example.

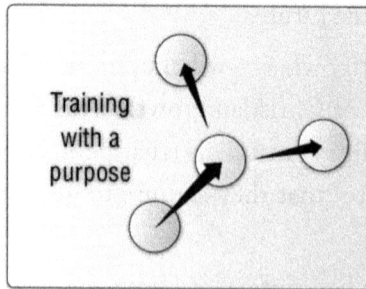

Training with a purpose

Whether we like it or not, new believer training is limited by time. Just as an infant quickly grows up and is weaned by the age of two, the new believer needs to be taught the basic truths of the faith right away. I suggest disciple makers to meet with new believers to discuss these truths at least seven to ten times **immediately** after they believe.

Those who are training pastors and evangelists must extend this vision of what God is desiring to do through the lives of the believers, including instructing more mature believers to train new believers. Unless this becomes one of our major goals of training, then those we train will become like I was—a new believer ignorant of how to train others, or even how to handle my own struggles.

The problem is much greater than this, however. For when we do not have this vision or knowledge of how to train others to care for new believers, we ruin the best opportunity to start training leaders. We neglect providing new believers what they need to grow and flourish.

Did you ever associate the problems in believers' lives stemming from poor training early on? What a shame that the church is often found criticizing believers for not spiritually growing up rather than repenting over their lack of personally providing biblical nurture and training for them.

"For though by this time you ought to be teachers, you have need again for someone to teach you the elementary principles of the oracles of God, and you have come to need milk and not solid food. For everyone who partakes only of milk is not accustomed to the word of righteousness, for he is a babe" (Hebrews 5:12-13).

Our challenge

In this age with an increasing number of voices offering advice, we need, like a mother to a newborn, to extend that crucially-needed one-to-one care and bring the needed milk of the Word into their lives.

I love hearing comments from people in our congregation, "I was so greatly helped by this or that brother. I'll never forget what I learned." May such comments be multiplied over the entire globe. Loving "child" training opens up the pathway to strong and vibrant Christian lives. As these disciples are cared for, then they will be in a position to train others.

Lessons

- Every new believer needs a more mature believer to personally disciple him or her.

- Without personal discipleship new believers go through many extra struggles and often leave the church.

- Those involved in evangelism and caring ministries must not only train counselors to personally disciple new believers but also to extend the vision of one day being used by God to train other new believers.

Memorize & Meditate

Hebrews 5:12-13

Assignment

➡ Have you mentored a new believer? When? Who?

➡ If not, why not?

➡ How did you train them? Note any materials or themes that might have been discussed.

➡ What problems did you face training new believers?

#28 Equipping New Believers

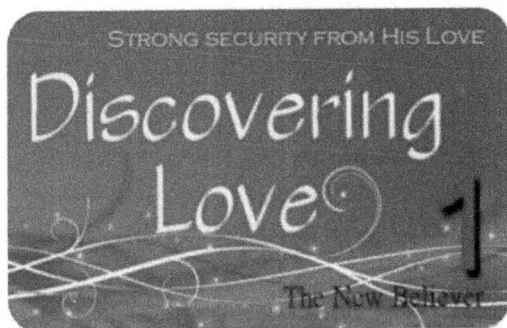

STRONG SECURITY FROM HIS LOVE

Discovering Love 1

The New Believer

Our care for new believers greatly influences the whole process of training. If we do not properly equip our leaders to disciple, then the lack of a good foundation for these new believers can't help but weaken the overall ministry. God's work will not be done in the manner and degree needed.

Proper training enables us to bring about the needed changes to equip upcoming leaders to train others in various areas of life. This chapter will provide ideas on how to train new believers and the importance of integrating this training with the life core.

The Life Core speaks about God's specific and personal work in the life of every genuine believer and the church as a whole. Regeneration starts a lifelong, relentless engagement of the Holy Spirit's sanctifying work in every believer.

He saved us, not on the basis of deeds which we have done in righteousness, but according to His mercy, by the washing of regeneration and renewing by the Holy Spirit, whom He poured out upon us richly through Jesus Christ our Savior (Titus 3:5-6).

Notice how the 'pouring out' of the Holy Spirit refers to God's unwavering and constant work as a flowing river in our lives.

God's work in the new believer

John the Apostle rightly discerned that the new believer has special needs, just like a little baby or toddler has. The family makes major time and financial adjustments to accommodate their little ones. For example, they are typically willing to use their limited resources on remodeling a room or buying needed food supplies for their precious, new child. John uses this analogy to increase our awareness of the critical need for nurturing the new believer–basics to sustain life.

One of the greatest challenges that we face training others to nurture new believers is the fact that we ourselves have not been personally discipled. We figure, "I turned out okay. It is not necessary." But we are blind to how much better things could have been.

Do we not see how unbelief runs rampant among our youth? They do not see the power of the gospel in their personal lives. Our greatest challenge is to show the relevancy of the gospel to each believer's life.

Our churches spend much time and money on bringing the gospel to the lives of others but hardly any on the nurturing of new believers. It is like the man who spends a lot of money on securing the best seed to grow a special crop, but after the initial excitement of seeing the initial sprouts, he forgets to water them!

Whether a church, seminary or training school, we must purposely:

(1) Convince God's people of the importance and need to train new believers,

(2) Equip them how to train new believers,

(3) Supply suggested materials they can use to train new believers, and

(4) Challenge them to train new believers with the whole birth-to-serving process in mind.

Convince others

If there are new believers around, then it becomes easier to convince God's people that we need to nurture them, but when the people around are hardened to the gospel, such as in some Western countries, it might not be a common thing to meet up with new believers. Finding opportunities to envision believers on discipling other new believers, therefore, becomes difficult. This needs to be tackled on two fronts (always include passionate prayer at every step).

First, we must seek the lost. Many Christians are ill-equipped, both in skill and vision, to reach out to the lost. (It seems much easier to criticize the world than covert them!) Give extra time, if necessary, to lead others to the Lord. Make evangelism part of *The Life Core* curriculum, if not a major thrust. (Note how The Flow diagram, Appendix 3, has a dotted line reminding us of the initial stream of life.) Second, we should look to the Lord to expand our opportunities of discipling beyond our one setting, such as our church, school or seminary. We need to go to where the need is. There are many distressed sheep out there that have lost their way. God's people must learn to work with the Lord to care and nurture them, as He leads.

Equip others

Once people are convinced that discipling new believers is important, we can easily equip them. Just like training in anything, those training must be familiar with the process. The teacher must first be familiar with training new believers, then they can equip others.

Some leaders are more equipped at doing this than others. Don't forget to use those especially gifted, in or outside your church, to do the training. I remember taking about fifteen people in a course through a new believer's booklet. I gave them a booklet with only an outline which they would fill in. This would later become their master copy to disciple others. I built up their vision along with the skill and knowledge training. They would later be able to use this to train others. (This is where I created the *3 X E: Discipling One-to-One* new believer training resource.)[8]

There are many ways to enhance this learning. One way to accomplish this is to demonstrate how it might work out through role playing in class. A monitor/leader must oversee the first discipleship training sessions. Either he accompanies the new trainee while discipling or carefully goes over the training experience after the first discipleship sessions. Remember, this does not need to be a one-time thing. We can ask the shy people to start with accompanying us and request that they take a part or share in the discipleship time. For example, when speaking on the Gospel and faith, they can share how Jesus saved them. They learn, some quicker, some slower, that God can use them to train others.

Mothers are able to physically feed their babies (very few exceptions) but more problematic is that they do not know how to handle some difficult circumstances. Spiritually nurturing is the same. We need to be right by their side to pass on suggestions in an encouraging way. Don't wait for them to ask you! You take time with these new disciplers so that they don't despair. Give them a great first time experience discipling others.

Supply others to train

There are an increasing number of discipleship training programs and materials. This is good. Some people are thinking

---

[8] 3 x E: Discipling One-to-One: www.foundationsforfreedom.net/Help/ Store/Intros/3xe_Discipling.html

about it. When I was young, there were only a few campus groups that had developed their own discipleship training booklets.

One major flaw was that they were not church-centered but primarily focused on an individual's own spiritual life. The theology of the church was not properly integrated. The value of individualism usurped the spot for love and service. Things are somewhat better, but there still remains some tension between church and parachurch organizations. They need to work together for a common purpose.

A few churches prepare their own materials. I would encourage this trend. Each church could customize their own new believer discipleship resources, even offering several versions for people with different needs. A larger printed booklet could be prepared for the elderly. Special language versions could be developed for ministering to immigrants or a picture version for the illiterate. (You can start with ours and remake it for yourselves!)

Most important, however, is the actual content. This book has discussed the concept of God's purposes for the three stages of discipleship but only briefly introduced the actual content to be considered. For further understanding in this area check out our three Discipleship Libraries.

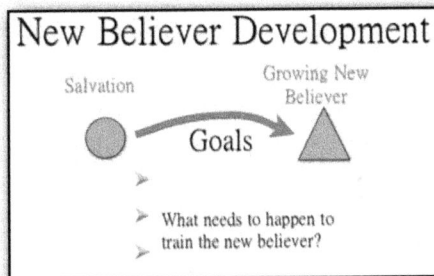

Specialized caring

Caring for the needs of the new believers must stand as a priority of the church. Just as a family shifts schedules and resources to care for the infant's needs, so the church must ensure proper care for the new children of God.

The new believer requires basic clarification of the gospel, nurturing from the Word of God, and help understanding how their new Father cares for them. The purpose is to strengthen their faith so they are properly grounded in the faith at this vulnerable time in life.

Their faith needs to be strengthened so that they are not easily led away but have clear enough understanding about sin, forgiveness, Christ, and faith, so that in their given circumstances, they are more deeply assured of God's constant love and provision for their lives.

If the new believer comes out of a partying environment, then they need further training on varying aspects of Christian life, community, and holiness. If they come from a background of legalism, then they need special clarification on salvation, sanctification, and the freedom of the gospel.

If another believer has problems being caught up in consumerism or with problems at home or work, then special instruction must help the new believer cope with these special issues that he or she is facing. Whatever 'world' they are rescued from, they will need an accompanying emphasis on that area. This is one reason one-to-one discipleship at this first stage of spiritual development is so important. We can provide specialized answers that would otherwise be neglected during a large group class. Let us not forget the basics, however. The focus for the new believer touches on the basics of Christian salvation. Stage two of Christian development helps these believers to rightly live in the world about them.

Integrate faith

Integrating an understanding of their new lives with what God is doing as a whole is critical. This complete picture explains the deeper truths that lay a foundation for their ongoing Christian lives. Let me provide two examples.

Identify their new desires for the Word of God. It is similar to a baby craving for his mother's milk. Help them realize this is their new life wanting and needing God's Word. Like eating food, this will be something ongoing, though the awareness of it is greater at this stage.

New believers also desire to be with other believers, to pray and to share God's Word with others. This is the Spirit of God excitedly working through their lives letting them know they are part of a larger spiritual family. As we regularly point out these things, new Christians begin to gain a good handle on God's involvement in their lives. All these smaller lessons form a larger picture of God's love for them. Remember to connect what is happening in them with why it is happening. God's Spirit is working in them. That life is growing and expressing itself.

God's constant love

God's love is constant and real. Even if we fail, God has provided a way to gain forgiveness through Christ; He is our advocate (1 John 2:1-2).

If we have not grown up in a good family, we often feel as if we have to prove ourselves or battle with feeling unloved by others. But with proper discipleship, new believers will grow by understanding God's constant love for them, despite their poor upbringings.

A sense of appreciation (the early formation of teaching of grace and mercy) deepens when they learn how to rightly appropriate Christ's undeserved forgiveness for their sins through Christ. They will see the great importance of Jesus Christ's loving work on the cross on their behalf, not through works or rituals of their own.

At each stage, God is building up foundational values upon which the next phase of development depends. Without a good grasp of God's love, new believers will have a hard time moving through the second stage of spiritual development.

The church's problems are largely inherited from an older generation of believers who did not disciple new believers. Dysfunctional begat dysfunctional.

Summary

Much more can be said, but in summary remember our need to adjust priorities to reinforce God's purposes for this first stage of training wherein we nurture new believers. Make sure we are effectively training God's people to care for these new believers.

These lessons are basic and essential, and yet ironically, greatly lacking in the church. Without this care, they will not gain the firm foundation of love and trust to properly grow in the second stage of Christian training. They won't become those believers that you had hoped them to be, but they will wobble about in their Christian lives.

The time has come for us to stop blaming new believers for being so fickle, and start providing the care God has instructed us to give them from the beginning.

The new believer stage is brief and should be implemented immediately. The devil is ready to destroy them. We must do our best to reach them first and guide them along. They are, for a short time highly motivated to study hard and grow, and it is so much more enjoyable to work along with new believers rather than trying to restore a defeated backslider to where he should be. Let's be proactive in doing God's will!

Lessons

- The church and all Christian training groups must personally and carefully disciple new believers.

- New believers must be trained with a view for the future, both in respect to their full development but also how God will use them to train other new believers.

- Customized material for the new believer must take into consideration the special needs they face in life.

Memorize & Meditate

Titus 3:5-6

Assignment

➡ Have you trained other new believers? Explain.

➡ What programs or materials would you use to train a new believer?

➡ Think of three new believers that you know of. If you would disciple them, what special needs do they face that you would need to take into consideration?

➡ If you are involved in leadership training, begin to store up customized and specialized lessons for your people to use to train others. Write down how far you are along and where you would like to be in this regard.

#29 Supporting Young Believers

Readying for combat

The teen has very different needs than the little child, just as a young believer has different needs from the new believer. The difference might only be two years' time, but much has changed in that time. This chapter focuses on training Christian young believers.

Challenge for the young believer

While the steps toward maturity quickly bring the young believer into new situations which are readying him or her for spiritual adulthood, they are not yet there. They need spiritual training to guide them through facing the least amount of distress as possible.

I am writing to you, young men, because you have overcome the evil one....I have written to you, young men, because you are strong, and the word of God abides in you, and you have overcome the evil one (1 John 2:13-14).

John again furnishes us with special insight from 1 John 2:12-14. He focuses us on the aspects of struggle, temptation, and learning from God's Word. The image of the person in spiritual armor from Ephesians 6 also comes to mind:

Put on the full armor of God, that you may be able to stand firm against the schemes of the devil. For our struggle is not against flesh and blood, but against the rulers, against the powers, against the world forces of this darkness, against the spiritual forces of wickedness in the heavenly places (Ephesians 6:11-12).

The important thing to remember is that this is not just something certain believers go through but what all believers will eventually encounter. This comprises a large part of their training.

Their success at this second stage is closely related to how well they were cared for during the first stage. New believer training enables them to gain the right perspective that God is always near to help them. It also helps them gain a good relationship with mentors. Without this awareness deeply planted inside them, they will not be able to easily trust God as they go through the young believer training. Doubts easily lead to discouragement and defeat, which in turn might bring despair, wondering if they ever will be victorious.

The knowledge that all spiritual 'teens' go through this stage makes it easier for the trainer. Let's get to know new friends or students that come to our church so that we can help them assess where they are on their spiritual journey. This will also help us develop special evaluative tools to know what the church can do to help them at their current stage of spiritual growth. What once was vague can be quite clear.

To be sure there are dangers of comparing oneself with others, but rightly presented, this spiritual growth chart can be used to help each believer evaluate him or herself and to encourage his or her companions rather than judging them. Our motive is to help people grow, not to criticize and compare.

The needs of the young believer

The new believer needs to learn basic truths about salvation, eternal assurance, etc. These truths build basic trust in God. John speaks about these. God our Father is there to care for us.

The young believer, however, must learn how to use God's Word on his own. He should no longer be spoon fed but ought to feed himself with God's Word. This transition will have a direct relationship on our training. We must enable the believer to gain the skills to create on-going spiritual disciplines along with fostering a sensitive and trusting heart ready to appropriate God's Word for themselves. For example, teaching people how to do inductive Bible studies will greatly help them in acquiring skills for more in depth studies, but we must remember not everyone has the same educational background for this.

The depth of the young believer's integration of God's Word into their lives will directly impact how well they learn how to ward off the evil one. Group teaching is possible here but mentoring is better for working with personal struggles. Establishing good working relationships enable us to monitor how people are doing through their different stages of development.

One's physical age can affect how quickly a believer might spiritually grow. A young child will take much longer than an adult to go through this young believer stage. This has to do with their ability to process information and the way they interact with others.

The goals for the young believer

The length of this second stage of discipleship, therefore, can differ, but generally speaking, it should take about three years. Some, or should we say many, unfortunately never grown out of it. They have never mastered the needed lessons. Their length of knowing Christ cannot be a gauge of spiritual maturity. We can deduct from John that the young believer has several major things to learn:

(1) Spiritually nurture themselves with God's Word (e.g. , regular and helpful quiet times).

(2) Comprehend key teaching from God's Word regarding areas such as victory over the devil through Jesus Christ's work on the cross.

(3) Consistently discern and overcome temptations that come into their lives.

It is hard, if not impossible, to say when a person becomes a teen and leaves behind the teenage years and attitudes. Since it is vague in the physical realm, we can allow it to be vague in the spiritual world too. There will be those times when he or she is still spiritually young but acts mature, and vice-versa.

It is more important to focus on the main goals for the young believer and identify what must happen to reach those goals. Our Lord is able to use all sorts of situations that we encounter to train us. Nothing is off limits. Be a learner. He doesn't waste a moment as our Master Trainer.

Raising up godly mentors

Our stage two training book highlights how a believer learns how to use God's Word to grow at this young believer stage.[9]

---

[9]Reaching Beyond Mediocrity: Faith's Triumph Over Temptation. (Both book and workbook/video training formats.)

Finding a godly mentor/teacher who believes we have overcome the evil one—not only in theory only but in a practical way—is extremely helpful.

Because many believers haven't been rightly trained, they just do not master these needed lessons of faith. The trainer must learn how to take these individuals and focus them on where they need to be as believers. If the mentor has not learned how to overcome temptations in one or more areas of his or her life, then the younger believer will be trained to doubt that God can help them too. This zaps rather than strengthens one's faith.

I remember taking counseling courses and reading many pastoral training books to help me gain confidence so I could personally grow in the areas in which I was struggling. These are things I should have mastered far earlier in my life.

There is a general unbelief in the church that believers can overcome the various personal struggles that they face. These struggles often have to do with the integrity of their lives and how they can focus on the needs of others rather than upon their own concerns. The 'victim' mentality presupposes there is no way of winning. Without a history of overcoming, mentors have no message of hope to offer but only unbelief and cover-up for those they train. Being open about one's failure is one matter, but has the mentor shared his or her victories?

Giving the greater vision

This is the reason we need to make this whole spiritual development chart available so that everyone, including mentors, can see where they are at in their spiritual journey. It stirs teachers, pastors, and trainers on to a faith that God can help them overcome their sinful behaviors such as looking at porn (really adultery), spiritual pride, anger, etc. We repudiate the increasing tendency to send believers with problems to 'specialists' who subdue problems with drugs or "psycho-babble." This might keep them from extreme behavior but cripples their spiritual response system. Why not show them how to overcome these things and learn how to trust God for these matters? Our aim is to build up the discernment of young believers so that they can see the evil one tempting them and know exactly how to respond. When they consistently do this, they will have moved into the third stage of spiritual growth, one that will continue all their days on earth.

Without faith in God's work at each stage, we will not reach the end goal of full maturity. But if we believe, somehow and someway, that God has purposed me and others to move through the second stage of spiritual maturity, then we be able to trust Him to get through. Our faith in God's work in us will keep us from giving up.

Lessons

- The young believer has a different growth trajectory than the new believer.

- The young believer must learn how to nurture himself in God's Word so that he can overcome a variety of temptations.

- There is a crisis in the church because older believers are not convinced that they can overcome any and every temptation (they have not grown through this stage). They lack faith.

- Although the steps to overcoming temptation are fundamental, young believers along with their trainers often cannot clearly delineate how to do this, and so believers sink into an unbelieving, lukewarm state.

Memorize & Meditate

Ephesians 6:11-12

Assignment

➡ Why do you think you are or are not a young believer? Give some reasons.

➡ How well are you equipped to train a young believer to overcome every sort of temptation?

➡ Are there areas that you have not overcome or would not know how to help someone else? What are they?

➡ Seek the Lord to restore your belief that His people can overcome and to show you how God's people can do this.

#30 Equipping Young Believers

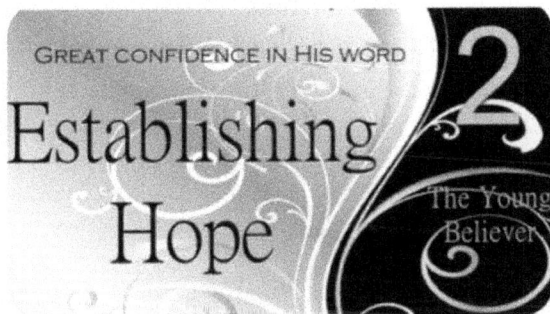

Let's discuss training for the young believer. Every little child will physically grow up, but many face a difficult time maturing. They can misunderstand so many things, especially if they grow up in unloving homes. The more dysfunctional their background, the more difficulties these young people face. Spiritually young believers face the same problems as young people do being brought up in dysfunctional homes.

Confusion abounds

Having trained and talked to many people preparing for ministry, I sense that not a few go to seminary largely to work through personal problems. They think that theology will make their personal struggles disappear.[10] They should have received the training to overcome these inner struggles in their churches and then, because of a calling, begin more official training.

---

[10] The answer is not theology but truth–truth believed upon. This problem again illustrates that what we know is not necessarily what we believe.

Unfortunately, the training they need at this second stage of discipleship is missing in most churches, and for that matter, in most seminaries. Counseling courses and majors have come into existence largely because the church has not properly instructed God's people in these areas.

I wonder, however, if those who sit in many such classes are truly being helped. The reason is that there is a great lack of faith as to where the Christian should be or how he should get there. Many counselors teach that one should tolerate a little anger and anxiety, but this is adopting a perspective so different from what is given to us in the scriptures. We want to eliminate anger, not just to manage it. [11]

God's goals are good

God has His goals and means, but the church has not adopted God's goals and does not rely on His means to help His people grow. The problem is not the world from which the new believers come but the lack of faith in the church and her leaders.

God wants all His people to receive great training so they can grow up into strong and godly people (see Ephesians 4:15-16). This training is not to be relegated to some professional with a state license in counseling. Believers increasingly assume one needs a doctorate degree to be able to help someone cope with basic spiritual struggles in life. This is so wrong.

Although churches should be training their people, many are not and therefore this instruction is needed in Bible Schools and seminaries. What pastor or missionary or Christian Educator, Youth Worker, single person, wife, etc., does not need to understand and live out righteous living? We all need to. Godly living is the core to Christ-like ministering. We need this

---

[11] Anger as an emotion is God-given, but we speak of the way our flesh hijacks anger to bring about much pain and bitterness (Eph 4:31).

teaching so that we can assure that all of God's people are spiritually strong and healthy.

Leaders also need training on how *The Life Core* needs to be integrated into their training ministries. They need to adopt God's goals of godly living and learn how to train others. Here are some goals of training the young believers. Each young believer needs to:

- Be fully equipped to spot temptation

- Understand the fundamental problem of temptation

- Observe how temptation relates to their sin nature and the world

- Acquire and use the truth to fight temptation

- Prioritize the place of forgiveness in their hearts

- Personally witness the power of God's Word

Young Believer Development

New Believer

Strong Young Believer

Goals

In what ways does the faith of the young believer need to grow?

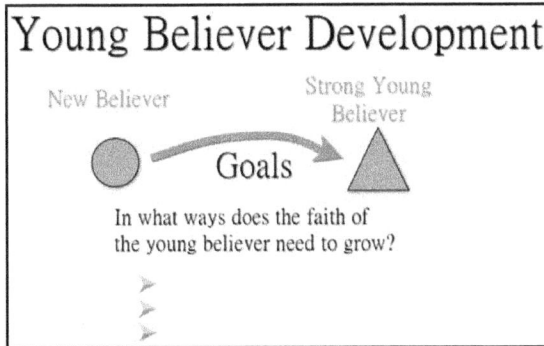

Faith accompanying our vision

John the Apostle stated the truth: young men have overcome the evil one. Both men and women of God have their victory secure. It is not something that could be, but something that is. When we allow the full power of God's Word into our lives, then our faith is strengthened, and we can discern Satan's lies, apply the truth, and stand firm.

For whatever is born of God overcomes the world; and this is the victory that has overcome the world--our faith (1 John 5:4).

Again, we need to stress that this is all part of a larger life core process. Spiritual life was given to us that we could consistently win over temptation (though that is not our end goal). Many counselors are not leading God's people to victory but instead only on how to cope with or to tolerate defeat. This is a far cry from God's purpose in the Gospel of Jesus Christ. God wants to give us consistent victory. We must refuse to give the evil one any foothold in our lives. God wants to give us consistent victory. We must refuse to give the evil one any foothold in our lives.

Advantages of training

In the beginning, of course, we need to regularly return to the power of the cross to find forgiveness and restoration. This is simply reminding us of God's amazing grace.

As the believer endures fight after fight, however, he is beginning to see how the evil one pins him down. Training for this stage should focus on how to ward off the evil one's schemes and through the power of God's Word to stand strong.

By implementing this training with every student, church member, attendee, etc., we boost the faith of each believer. This is not a simple religious recitation of 'I believe' but learning how to take God's Word and use it to overcome the evil one.

Is this not the purpose of God for each believer's life? Why is it that most believers never get through this stage? Many pastors and teachers tell me that they are still at this second stage. If they are still there, then they have not yet matured in their faith to train others about how to escape, at least in the areas they feel weak.[12] Worse yet are those leaders which are convinced it is not possible to live godly lives and overcome temptation.

Learning how to train

You might be wondering how we can train in this area? Where can we learn how to put these behaviors and characteristics into practice? The training is personally challenging but not complicated or expensive. The Apostle John has done a wonderful job at targeting the key areas on which we need to focus.

The basic principles are explained in the first four chapters of our 'Reaching Beyond Mediocrity: Faith's Triumph Over Temptation.' It is built on the assumption that God has already made us overcomers and that God is working on our behalf in this spiritual warfare in which we're engaged to better reflect His holy image. The later chapters use these principles to show how they empower us to overcome major personal problems like anger, lust, and pride.

If one does not learn how to properly handle 'little' sins, such sins will become occupiers, eventually destroying him or her. Think of the many pastors that have blown up their ministries with anger, lust, or bitterness. The needed protection takes place deep in the heart through God's Word. "Watch over your heart with all diligence, for from it flow the springs of life" (Proverbs 4:23).

Growing up

This training does not take long. Just as a person should grow through the teenage years, a young believer should grow to full maturity in just a matter of a few years.

---

[12] This is one big reason that the church goes from strong to weak. What one leader does not learn to overcome, he tolerates and promotes lesser standards to ease his conscience.

I generally say it takes about three years to grow through this stage. The principles can be learned more quickly if the disciple is already knowledgeable of God's Word. The problem is not time or expense. The biggest problem is to persuade teachers and pastors to believe this is what God wants and can do in each believer's life. We are not suggesting some type of magical or miracle healing process to be followed, but are putting forth clear biblical principles that work!

Clarifying our vision

Think for a moment. What is your personal belief about average believers? Do you think they can grow into full spiritual maturity? Are they able to withstand every temptation?

What if we personally could believe that God wants us to consistently overcome every temptation so that we do not need to fall. Would that not be an awesome bit of news? The church is lukewarm because it has given up hope that real change can occur.

What kind of people are we graduating from our training schools and seminaries? What kind of leaders are we producing in our churches? Are we satisfied with their spiritual maturity? In most cases, the unfortunate answer is 'no.' The reason is simple. We have not trained them in the manner that God's word directs. Due to their learned unbelief and defeat, they will in turn train others to not seek for personal victory. It is imperative that our leaders learn to live by the truth of God's Word and to teach others to do likewise.

Our church congregations are in such a mess, not because they can't change, but because they do not believe they can be changed. Although addictions form extra barriers to overcome, they can likewise be leaped over as we consistently apply these principles with a heart of faith.

Implementation of God's vision

How do we implement this in our schools and churches? Some instruction can be taught in classes, but small group and individual mentoring is key to identifying personal struggles and then being able to show how the victory process works.

People often do not like to publicly acknowledge their weaknesses and sins. They might not have problem talking about certain sinful problems, but others are hidden behind the scenes, including negative reactions and sinful thought patterns. Many sinful responses like an unforgiving spirit are embedded into our lives early on from our childhood so that our familiarity with them overrides their warnings of pain, emotional withdrawal, and mistrust.

How do I know these things? God's Word has told us so. I have seen what happens when we do not live by His greater principles. Our lives are characterized by defeat and failure rather than testimony and victory. On the other hand, I have experienced the awe at seeing the power of His truth working itself out in my life and others. Personal victory goes a long way in establishing effective trainers. You can't really pass something on that you don't have yourself. Schools of ministry along with churches must establish victorious trainers to implement the 2 Timothy 2:2 process.

God is cheering us on to victory. He has made it so we can overcome. Now we need to obey Him, grow through this stage, and move onto maturity where He has greater plans for us. The quality and quantity of our fruitful service greatly depends on how well we do at this second stage.

If the church would have these truths integrated into their training for all believers, God's people would be strong in their faith! Revival would be at hand. Families would be restored. There would be plenty of great leaders. Without proper shaping of the heart and mind, though, we are only perpetuating our problems while the evil one's dark ways and mindset seeps into our lives. True training must include the establishing of strong godly lives, without which there is no true love.

Lessons

- Many believers go about as defeated Christians because they are not charmed by the power and glory of God's Word working in their lives.
- God has given the church the means to live holy lives by regularly overcoming sin and affirming the truth of the cross for her failures.
- When the church embraces the faith to overcome temptation and sin, then she will learn how to depend on her powerful God and find revival.
- Training must come from leaders who have seen the power of God working in their lives.

Memorize & Meditate

1 John 5:4

Assignment

➡ Identify one weakness in your life and the steps needed to overcome it. Are you actively working on overcoming that problem? Can you communicate this process to others?

➡ Name several major sins you see in others. Explain the steps needed to help each of them gain hope and faith to step out of those sins.

➡ Does your church or school tolerate immaturity and sinful attitudes/behaviors in the leaders it is developing? How should this problem be approached?

#31 Mentoring Maturing Believers

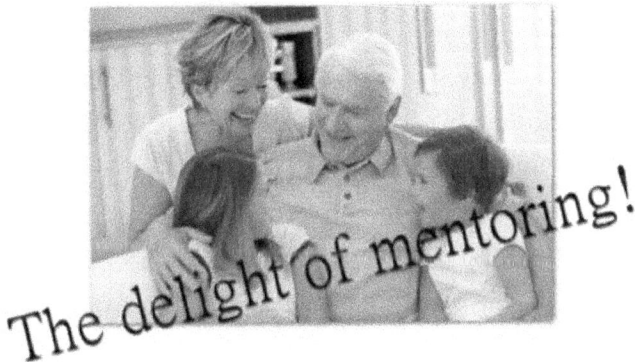

The delight of mentoring!

One of the biggest challenges to properly think about this third spiritual stage of growth, described by John as 'fathers', is that it has culturally become improper to describe oneself as a mature believer. This mindset portrays a false sense of humility and prevents His people from having a much needed biblical approach to life. Do you know any fathers that deny themselves being a father, "Oh, you think so. But I really am not a father"? This scene is ridiculous (especially when you see his two little boys pulling at his trousers requesting something). Being a father is a normal stage of life, nothing to be shamed about.

Properly handling pride

The problems of pride and the snare of thinking that we 'have arrived' is certainly a great problem, but if we get a proper look at the father stage, we will discover that the biblical perspective has its own way of dealing with pride.

Comparison is a problem with sinful mankind. Man's prideful tendency thinks of him or herself as better than others. The biblical view, however, has us:

(1) Increasingly adopt God's standards and goals

(2) Seek God to continually mentor us in godliness

(3) Be trained to better help those around us.

Can you see the difference? By seeking growth, we admit that we have room for growth and further maturity. By focusing on serving others, we no longer compare ourselves to others. This is the proper spirit behind this third stage of the spiritual fathers. If anything, we should be crying out for those many Christians around us have not become fathers but ensnared somewhere along the way.

Jesus said it was fine and proper to think of oneself as mature. "The soil produces crops by itself; first the blade, then the head, then the mature grain in the head" (Mark 4:28). This last stage is where we should expect to bear fruit. In contrast, how tragic our lives are when we produce no godly fruit because of self-indulgence, perhaps by wasting time watching videos or playing games. There is, perhaps, no greater sin than for a father to disregard his children's needs while using his money and time to lavishly treat himself. It happens, but what a tragic affair.

In the first stage we saw how the little child was very dependent on the parents, even for the basic needs of life. In the same way, we find it only proper that each believer grows in Christ until maturity where they lead others to Christ and help them in their spiritual walk. If no one cares for the new and young believers, they will flounder in their faith. This is the spirit of fatherhood—caring for those around you, and at a minimum, those that you lead to Christ.

This third stage is where we train believers to learn to properly care for others. Included in this training, while developing a foundation for serving, is understanding how to cultivate a deeper and more intimate life with God. As fathers, men and women of faith, mature in these things. They develop into leaders who are willing to oversee the needs of the church as a whole, as well as minister to other individual believers around them.

From a parent's perspective

I have eight children with a range between the oldest and youngest of 22 years. Right now, I have four teens. This trend will continue for a number of years yet! Some are getting close to graduating from high school while others still haven't settled into their adult lives. We are not in a hurry, but we do constantly pray that they would get the needed education that allows them to find a good job so that they in turn can care for their own family. As parents we desire more for them than anyone else.

God as our 'Parent' likewise desires us to move on into full maturity. Maturity rings with a sense of fulfillment with respect to what God has designed for our lives. The third stage of spiritual development is unlike Hinduism whose most spiritual men detach themselves from their family and the 'real' world, spending the rest of their lives seeking spiritual enlightenment. Quite the contrary, the mature Christian believer seeks further intimacy with God so that he or she can properly engage in serving others.

People in the world perhaps serve just to receive a financial or emotional reward. God's people serve because they have been overwhelmed with appreciation to God for His work in their lives. They seek to please Him and care for others. Some Christians are called to pastor, but all believers are meant to grow up caring for others. The pastors equip everyone to serve (Ephesians 4:11-12).

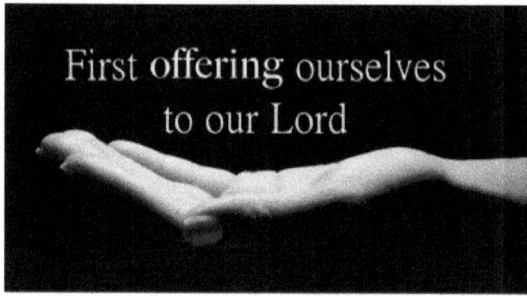

First offering ourselves
to our Lord

With a heart to serve

How does our perspective of serving affect our lives? The vision of service should be deeply integrated in the mind and heart of the believer. This is a big challenge in the various societies throughout the earth where those in authority feel that it is now time to be served. This selfishness is subtle but very real in our post–modern world. We look forward to retirement where we get to indulge in our own pleasures, without any sense of responsibility to others.

Paul rebuked those who focus on their own spirituality without concern for others, "Brethren, do not be children in your thinking; yet in evil be babes, but in your thinking be mature" (1 Corinthians 14:20).

Learning to effectively train

As trainers we need to carefully observe what is needed by those around us and provide whatever specialized training is necessary. Some churches are looking for discipleship programs. Programs are typically regimented and stiff, often not allowing for God's individual leading and input. Good resources are important, but time must be spent with individuals to see how the Lord is leading the person. Many resources such as video training seminars may be utilized, but we must always also include special times alone before the Lord.

Just this morning, during my quiet time before I wrote this, I was seeking the Lord about preparations for an overseas training trip. The Lord prompted me to write a note to some of my brothers there to clarify some issues. When I got to my computer, the issue had been confirmed by an email from our coordinator there stating the very same thing. God nudged my heart and then confirmed it. The decision had financial demands, but because God was in it, I can trust that He will provide the need. This way my faith was built up for greater things. Most of these heart lessons are learned in private with the Lord.

The goals for mature believers

Train mature believers how to:

➡ Seek intimacy with God

➡ Dive deeper in His Word

➡ Wrestle with deep personal struggles

➡ Persevere when others have given up

➡ Be believing when others doubt

➡ Be pure while living in an impure society

➡ Demonstrate God's love through serving others

➡ Kindly confront others as needed

The genuine believer never dares to stop growing. We grow in our relationship with God, aspiring to be like Jesus and better serve others. As a trainer or mentor, we are always looking to God on how to best foster development in one or more areas of our lives.

Lessons

- Believers should dream of being spiritually 'grown up', where they can be close to God and empowered by Him to serve those around them.
- God does want to bear fruit through our lives. This largely happens as spiritually mature believers see God's Spirit wonderfully working through their lives.
- Our training must not only instill this full vision for the believer but equip him or her to stay close to God and serve others.

Memorize & Meditate

1 Corinthians 14:20

Assignment

➡ Are you a mature believer? What evidence do you have to back up your answer?

➡ What challenges do you have to stay close to God?

➡ Have you ever experienced 'burn–out' where one feels spiritual dry and unable to serve as one used to? How did you handle it? How would you advise another to deal with this situation?

#32 Equipping Mature Believers

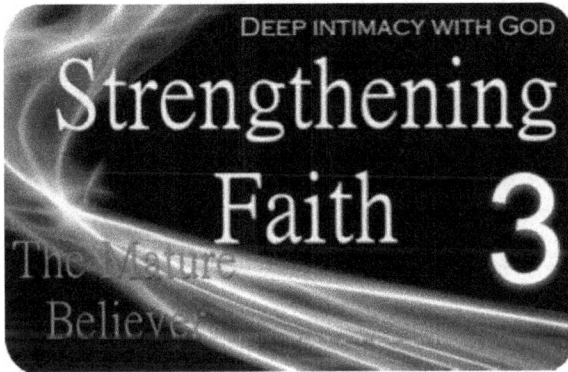

Training those in the third stage of a Christian's spiritual growth is significantly different from the first two stages.

Clarifying the goals for the fathers

The focus of the first two levels is to help the believer pass through those stages. According to John in 1 John 2:12-14, there is no fourth stage here in our earthly experience. This fact changes the way we approach growth at this level. So while in stages one and two, the believer focuses on goals that enable him or her to step onto the next stage, the believer in the third stage adopts goals for ongoing spiritual development within that stage.

Some dangers exist at this level. We might think of the elder who has been in control at his church for twenty or more years and is spiritually 'stuck' in his spiritual growth. Or consider the believer who thinks being faithful means sitting in the same pew for thirty years. And, of course, there is the heavy discipline that Moses received from the Lord for striking the rock rather than speaking to it (Numbers 20:11-12).

These problems can be solved by properly understanding growth at this third level of Christian development. Spiritual development will continue to unfold as we seek ways to maintain and grow in our intimacy with God through Christ. Even adults grow in their maturity, wisdom, compassion, and in the fullness of Christ (Ephesians 4:13).

Let us be aware, however. It is always much easier to train a new believer to reach the third level than to retrain those, stuck in their ways, who think they are grown up though they aren't.

Maintaining our growth

Although the word 'maintain' does not conjure up words of development, it does refer to consistently prioritizing certain spiritual disciplines in one's life. Prayer, for instance, that close intimate discussion with God can and should grow. Like personal Bible study, it needs to continue deepening.

These points where we are tempted to waver, slide into lukewarmness, or disobey also serve as the places where we further develop our commitment to God's purposes in our lives. Those at this third level are repeatedly being asked by the Lord, "What or who is most important in your life?" Our responses reveal whether we are seeking Him with all of our heart or not.

The test of perseverance

There are a few kings who did well early on in their service but later became prideful and idolatrous. These dangers, however, also are the very opportunities to affirm our commitment, make the right decisions, and keep on the path. There are many verses exhorting us to 'hold' on to the measure of growth that we have experienced:

> *Let us hold fast the confession of our hope without wavering, for He who promised is faithful (Hebrews 10:23).*

So then, brethren, stand firm and hold to the traditions which you were taught, whether by word of mouth or by letter from us (2 Thessalonians 2:15).

But examine everything carefully; hold fast to that which is good (1 Thessalonians 2:15).

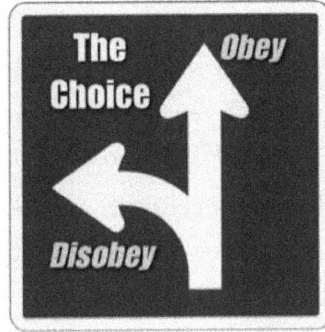

I am coming quickly; hold fast what you have, in order that no one take your crown (Revelation 3:11).

The mature believer should be careful to keep a fervent heart for the Lord. This is difficult. He or she will face times of disappointment, abundance, doubt, power, depression, fame, bitterness, grief, suffering, and perhaps persecution. Each becomes a situation in which we need to take the truths of old and again commit ourselves to live out God's ways.

Growing further

The great thing about spiritual life is that there is no end to the potential in growth. Paul expresses it well:

Not that I have already obtained it, or have already become perfect, but I press on in order that I may lay hold of that for which also I was laid hold of by Christ Jesus (Phil 3:12).

Paul realizes that his spiritual development and remaining life is not only for himself but for the Lord to work His purposes out through his life for others (Philippians 1:22-24). He wants to obtain all those large and small things that the Lord has planned for him.

Integration at the third level

When we think about John's exhortations in 1 John 2:12-14 for each of the three levels, we begin to more clearly focus on the growth that takes place during that stage of spiritual growth. This is also true with this third stage of Christian living. We are not just being religious, though from the outside it might look that way. We renew our purpose of knowing Christ and have Him live out His purposes through our lives.

Burnout occurs if we are not careful. Service becomes routine and dry if we do not often refresh ourselves in the Lord's presence. Notice how Paul reminds the Christians in Rome, "Not lagging behind in diligence, fervent in spirit, serving the Lord" (Romans 12:11).

The purpose for which we carry out these things must not be forgotten, either in our busy lives or desperate situations. Jesus is the ultimate example, showing the relationship between devotion and service:

I am the vine, you are the branches; he who abides in Me, and I in him, he bears much fruit; for apart from Me you can do nothing (John 15:5).

Notice the theme of life in Jesus' words: vine, branches, abides, bear, and fruit. Each word reminds us of the intimate relationship that we have if we are to continue to see the life of God worked out through ours in a purposeful way.

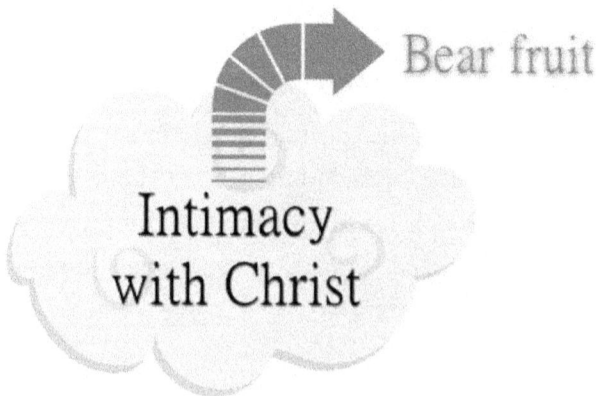

Bear fruit

Intimacy
with Christ

A look at training materials

Training at this stage requires developing more insight as to how Satan cleverly tempts believers, as well as fostering an intimate relationship with the Lord. From this comes both increased devotion and fruitfulness. In many cases, believers simply have not been able to maintain regular devotional times. As a result, they become 'apart' from Christ and cannot grow, becoming listless. Good training helps:

- The process of always having significant quiet times

- The way to restore good quiet times after a lapse

- The path to gain insights from difficult passages

- The means of listening to God from the scriptures

Many of these processes are simply not focused on in typical church or seminary training. We put the blame on people for not knowing how, rather than providing the great training our Lord would love to give them.

Special focus is also needed on the whole area of fruitfulness. Maturity produces fruit. Jesus not only expects us to bear fruit, but that it remains (John 15:16).

In most cases we measure our ministries by their fruitfulness. This is good, but it is important to keep a broader perspective of growth at this third stage. Just remember that fruitfulness is not always seen at every segment of this stage of Christian growth, such as when one is enduring hardship. The fruit from Jesus' sufferings only became apparent later after His resurrection.

There are many good books to foster Christian fervency and optimize our service. This is a great blessing for our age where we can 'meet' another strong believer through their training, books, and audio/videos. We can require books to be read, studies to be done, but as we move up into deeper intimacy with

Christ, we will see that many of the most important lessons cannot easily be tested or graded. This, no doubt, is one reason they often are neglected in schools.

A practical look

Mentoring at this stage is best when in small groups or one-to-one, a place everyone can openly share. The great aspect about discipleship is that even when a believer might be traveling a lot or in a church that does not do discipleship, he still can easily disciple another.

For example, on this third level, just find one or two brothers (or sisters if you are a sister) and find one common need. Often I ask the person what area he would like to grow in. I also share how I would like to see him grow in another area (e.g., listening to God, exploring a Bible book, etc.). Time is split between praying, sharing, and discussing the two areas. One can meet practically anywhere and at any time!

In the following chapters, we will reflect further on this development and what it means in formal training institutions, as well as informal ones such as churches where there are no degrees (but neither is there tuition!).

Lessons

- This third level of spiritual growth differs from the prior ones because its goal is to thrive within this stage rather than pass through it.

- Dangers that threaten our growth can be avoided by focusing on what God is doing through our lives at any given stage.

- The trainer equips each believer to carry out God's preplanned works He has for him, remembering that they can be done only through a growing intimacy with Christ and through God's grace.

- Christian training must do much more to prepare believers to grow in this third area of development.

Memorize & Meditate

Philippians 3:12

Assignment

➡ Write down three Christian life stories (yours or others) that have helped you in your spiritual growth. Explain how each helped you.

➡ Have you ever faced burnout, a dried up faith, etc.? Pick one situation and reflect how it came about. How was it finally resolved?

➡ Are you at the third level of maturity? Explain.

➡ What are your biggest challenges to maintaining a vibrant faith?

➡ Have you mentored anyone at the third level of spiritual development? What did it look like?

(4) Implement the Life Core

Chapters 33-40

#33 The Chief Purpose

Remembering Our End Goals

The Life Core has identified what the Lord's purposes are in believers' lives and how, in various settings, to deepen the flow of God's power, spurring on life transformation of God's people.

God's purposes or ours?

God is seeking to bring about that growth. When we go counter to His direct purposes, in ignorance or not, God's special life-changing work will only occur sporadically by His grace. But if by careful deliberation we adopt His purposes for our own, then we will see His power constantly at work.

Each school, church, family, and person needs to carefully examine its own situation in light of God's goals and make the needed adjustments. Good assessments must consider the present desires for such training as well as the consequences of not having closely worked with God on current programs and projects.

While most churches and other Christian institutions were established with solid purposes, many have been hijacked or have drifted away. If a church is not seeking God's goals or bearing fruit, then how can it be so sure it has not been broken off from the vine (John 15:1-6)? Many have started off with noble goals but have strayed from their course. This trend often occurs by focusing on what others expect rather than upon what God is trying to do.

God will not evaluate us by the number of our graduates or how long we survived but by the end product. Are God's people transformed and ready to be used of God to change others? Perhaps Christ will ask us, "To what degree did you enable my people to desire to be like me and serve others?"

If we examine our end results with our goals, we will no doubt find some completion of these goals. That is good, but the more we are able to fix our attention and major efforts on God's purpose of spiritual development, the more effective the equipping will become, shown in increased fruitfulness.

The relentless pursuit

God demands commitment to work with Him and this requires an ongoing pursuit of what He thinks is important. God does not want to be conceptually known but personally known and trusted. Each man and woman must gain his and her own trust in God. That trust is established through ongoing, often repetitive experiences, where the individual sees how God comes through for them in difficult times. Listen to how David's words.

> *I love you, O Lord, my strength. The Lord is my rock and my fortress and my deliverer. My God, my rock, in whom I take refuge; My shield and the horn of my salvation, my stronghold (Psalm 18:1-2).*

What do we see but a strong personal confidence in God Himself? David, though a mighty and clever warrior, discovered God's power and mercy through numerous life experiences. God wants to do the same with each genuine believer in his own context. Life is God's training school.

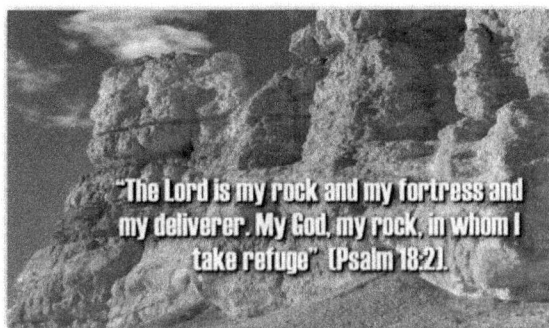

"The Lord is my rock and my fortress and my deliverer. My God, my rock, in whom I take refuge" (Psalm 18:2).

Avoiding confusion

Although we are aware of this process, the way to intertwine this with our training programs has been difficult. The development of our personal lives is hard to test and measure. The modern world, with its many regulatory agencies and official hoops to jump through, make improvements difficult. Sometimes it is not just governmental agencies, but our own church or accreditation groups specializing in helping us gain and maintain our qualifications. That is normally helpful, but at the same time, they constrain us to evaluate our institutions from their criteria rather than God's.

Tension mounts as our goals vary from the Lord's. He puts pressure on us to conform to His standards and expectations. It is helpful to clarify this process. The Lord might have us somehow break out of the system by special guidance and wisdom, but often He works with us right within the existing system.

The Life Core helps provide various ways to integrate God's spiritual development training with our present training methods. Below we will share some ideas on how to do this. For clarity purposes, we will refer to the professional college level training schools for full-time ministers but much is applicable to other situations. Just keep your church, life, etc., in mind as you read each point.

Characteristics of the Life Core

Here are some fundamental characteristics of this approach that are important to keep in mind:

➡ Intellectually stimulating

Two life analogies have been introduced, one regarding the source of life and the second describing the development of life (see appendix 1). Each analogy provides awareness of fundamental spiritual truths. The more we ponder upon them, the deeper the insights we gain of the invisible but real world of spiritual life.

Not too long ago, before man could explore the ocean's bottom, we thought it to be devoid of life. We now know that the deep ocean bottom is teeming with life and presents a vast new field of exciting exploration. The richness of studying God's purposes and ways in this manner is that it fosters meditation, wonder, and increased desire to learn and know God, who gives us this life.

Contrast this with studies on a religion like Buddhism or a study of some historical period. In the end, they reflect man's distortion, whereas *The Life Core* brings us to the very source of our lives, that which is good, right, thriving, and enabling. Indeed, the center of life itself is Christ in us (1 John 5:20)!

➡ Easily evaluated

To be honest, certain parts of the cycle of development are difficult to measure, but those in stages one and two can be more easily identified and evaluated. Having said this, we are not recommending to avoid control of accrediting agencies, even though they tend to focus on numbers and degrees rather than real change in the lives of the students.

Instead, we use these measurements to guide us in producing a worthwhile training program.

➡ Personally rewarding

Classes tend to wear teachers and students down. Heavy stress on academics gives little room for nurturing the spiritual life. When the garden soil becomes compressed, the plant root systems have a very difficult time expanding. As a result, there is little growth. Students relate that this problem exists even in our best seminaries.

Both professors and students are weighed down with the intellectual demands of the semester's work. They have precious little time for their own spiritual lives. The opposite should be true. When the focus can turn on genuine growth, accompanied by intellectual stimulation, everything becomes more meaningful and personally significant.

➡ Empowering and enlivening

All our learning must be brought back into the main, interpretative framework of life. The student does not only need the knowledge that is being thrusted at him but to nurture that life from God. The better a student is able to relate what they are learning with their inner lives, the more one can say they have genuinely learned.

Course knowledge is not only better comprehended, but internalized, when knowing how it relates to life and ministry. If they are incorporating life's core concepts simultaneously with their intellectual and practical studies, then they can regularly scrutinize what place it bears on what God is doing in their own lives and the lives of others. Courses become increasingly aligned to God's purpose and means. This insight excites and empowers.

➡ God-focused and Spirit-aided

There are many dangers that students face, but having theology, the study of God, replace knowing God is the greatest stumbling block. When we give proper focus, however, on God's glory and purpose, then other things can fall into place.

Without this chief goal of a thriving life with God, other goals will become overwhelmingly controlling.

➡ Fruit that endures

Our society needs transformation, but these needed changes come about through the intimacy God's people have with God rather than through the degrees they have gained. When adequate time and focus on spiritual transformation is not provided, then the inner growth is squelched and the fruit drops off before it can fully develop.

Careful examination

We are not just examining what happens to the students during their Bible school or seminary training, but afterwards. The enemy is always active, but the right training can go a long way to protect God's people from his devices.

Jesus said good works (i.e., His works) derive from communion with Him (John 15:5). By emphasizing the skills, character, and spiritual disciplines needed, we can further integrate this passion and way of life into the student, thus better preparing him or her for the real world. Paul summarized this change that we need to be fostering.

> But the fruit of the Spirit is love, joy, peace, patience, kindness, goodness, faithfulness, gentleness, self-control; against such things there is no law (Galatians 5:22-23).

Although different words are used, we need to be careful to focus on the quality of fruit that we seek. Good fruit is characteristic of those who live in God's presence. They are indelibly bound together.

Summary

A special emphasis on spiritual growth along with its clear path of development is necessary to retain biblical perspectives during the tough years of preparing for ministry.

Our goals of this life transformation program must seek for the greatest fruit to be born from the lives of its students. Otherwise, this life will be snuffed out rather than implanted in the lives of others. Christianity in many cases has become just another philosophy or religion, something to live with but nothing to live for. Returning to the life core brings us back to God and His life-generating powers.

Lessons

- God initiates influence for good upon us by challenging us to focus on His standards and expectations.
- The values found in the life core are rich and worthy to be prioritized.
- While we might look for these personally rewarding elements, nothing is more special than to discover how the training is a means by which God brings us and others closer to Him.

Memorize & Meditate

Galatians 5:22-23

Psalm 18:1-2

Assignment

➡ Do you have a life goal? What is it? (If not, write one out.) Does it involve knowing God in a deeper and more intimate way?

➡ What are the chief goals and aims of the school or church that you are attached to? Carefully read them. How do they compare with God's greater goals? Explain.

➡ Read through Psalm 18 and notice how David was deeply impacted by God's work in his life. Share two instances where you can share God has become 'my strength', 'my shield' or 'my...."

#34 The Inner Workings

The great importance of integrating spiritual transformation into our fixed schedules remains a formidable task. In this chapter, we will suggest one or more models for doing this.

The need for refocusing

Paul summarized his goals as "holding fast the word of life," that is, allowing Christ's Word to actively energize and guide all his thoughts, decisions, and attitudes.

> *Do all things without grumbling or disputing; that you may prove yourselves to be blameless and innocent, children of God above reproach in the midst of a crooked and perverse generation, among whom you appear as lights in the world, holding fast the word of life, so that in the day of Christ I may have cause to glory because I did not run in vain nor toil in vain (Philippians 2:14-16).*

Paul reexamined his thoughts and actions in light of God's call upon his life. Schools, churches, Christian businesses, and individual Christians must do likewise. They will be outwardly shaped by their own forms, language, styles, and time. That is fine. Down deep, however, nothing can replace the fact of God's life track, that deliberate design to reach its full potential and expression in our lives and institutions.

Our chief difficulty is to know how to properly place this Life Core at the heart of our training. In the garden, plants placed too close to each other will stifle overall growth. In order to gain the room needed, we must prioritize space so that the individual plant can get the right amount of light and air. This may mean fewer plants. This priority of place becomes a message to God and others what our chief purpose is, quality over quantity.

'Not what but who'

We must come to the realization that it is the God-initiated change of individuals that becomes the core aspect of our training. Without this key component, effective training falls short.

Perhaps, we have not possessed a way to focus on the change of the individual. We hope to provide two possible models here, though we prefer the first, at least in the initial stage.

Again, we are keeping a Christian school in mind as we speak here, but this can equally be applied to your church, parachurch organization, or individual life as needed. There are two choices:

(1) Keep the life core training as a separate developmental program–that runs along a more general agenda.

(2) Integrate the spiritual transformation program into an existing curriculum or program.

Each has its challenges. Let me explain the first. The other will become more apparent and briefly discussed as we understand the first. This will give better clarity to what the life core might look like in the church and elsewhere.

Keep separate with its own identity

Maintaining the life core's own identity is important to clarify its goals, to properly connect to other training courses, and to ensure its full development.

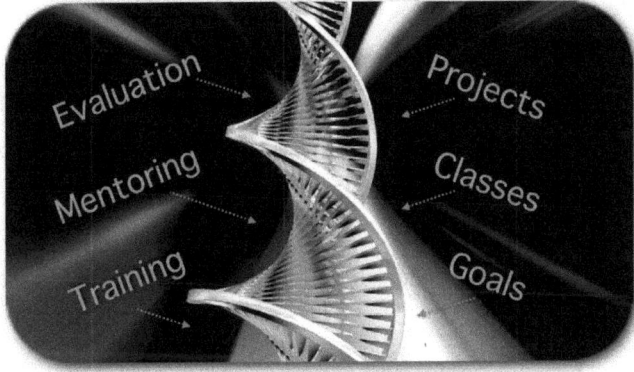

The Life Core diagram

The spiral represents the central core of our lives and institutions, even our theological colleges. God's purposes and life-giving source remains central. Our duty remains to keep our courses, decisions, etc., constantly influenced by God's presence. Our institution's purposes, training, classes, etc., must remain constrained by God's own purposes. The degree we can successfully do this determines success in God's eyes. (See appendix 4 for an expanded diagram.)

God's source of life, then, animates every aspect of our spiritual development. In practical terms, consider how the Holy Spirit works in each believer, perfecting what He has started (Phil 1:6). So likewise, we must integrate our courses and programs with God's inner workings.

By keeping the spiritual focus separate, it helps clarify our end goal and gives us an understanding of each level of development. Let us assume we are incorporating this into a three-year training school. Each component listed below is crucial to proper implementation.

The Goal

The end goal will never vary, though it can have various descriptions. We strive for the full development of each believer. By one's growing intimacy with Christ, he or she will be a vehicle through which God fully carries out His purposes.

Many would hardly deny these high end goals as something they are working towards, assuming godly interests and abilities, but it is important to assure that this development is taking place. By accompanying the large perspective with the goals of the three levels, we have some way of assuring others and ourselves that the expected spiritual transformation is taking place.

The starting place

Every student (or member if one is thinking about a church) is at a certain place when he or she begins. Often there are entrance tests that evaluate a person's Bible knowledge and personality. Although these have their place, we need to primarily focus on one's spiritual development. By using certain criteria at each of the three stages, we can test or hold discussions to help that student understand where he or she is growth-wise and where there are opportunities for further growth.

The spiritual maturity of an individual is not necessarily the same as intellectual acumen. Jesus didn't criticize the Pharisees for their lack of intellectual knowledge. They had an acceptable approach towards the Bible (compared to the Sadducees), but because of spiritual deadness and reliance on appearances, they did not properly view and apply the scriptures to their lives.

> Our first challenge is to evaluate where a person is;
> our second is to envision where he or she is to go,
> and our third is to help him or her reach there.

By identifying these points of growth early on and holding such conversations with them, we help the student (or member in our church) take steps in the right direction.

The planting of such seeds of hope shows that we expect the student to grow, not just in Bible or general knowledge, but in their spiritual lives with Christ. Our faith for them starts to shape their expectations and focus.

The development

Our goal is not to provide a generic map for each believer. This just isn't the way real life works. Each one has a different starting place. We do, however, want to see growth in certain areas. These common factors allow us to teach these truths and communicate them to others.

Perhaps, some will have issues of controlling anger. They will have different circumstances and triggers than others with a similar problem, and yet, the solutions will be similar. By taking time to discuss these things with the students, they will begin to focus their minds on it as something that needs to and can be addressed.

Personal mentoring will play a key role but classes or special seminars can also play a part. Perhaps, we can enhance the training of more spiritually mature students by having them train younger believers.

Special decisions will need to be made regarding those who do not really seem to know the Lord. We do this in churches with interviews before baptism. Schools will also wisely make this part of their evaluative process. Life is not present in the unbeliever so growth is impossible. Though with a believer, the signs of life might be difficult to see, life is still present and we have great hope for their development if they are open to it.

By clarifying our goals with the students, they will exclude themselves if they cannot identify with the schools goals.[13] (This implies that we should make our goals and methods clear and attractive.) By uninterested students excluding themselves, we are able to build up a greater unified focus for the school (or church).

Identifying specific goals

Depending on where the students are in their spiritual journey, we need to carefully work with them to help identify their next steps of spiritual development.

Classes (new or redesigned) can help with some of this training. We only need to assure the students think about their lives in this way. This is achievable by giving them 'life projects' or study assignments challenging them to see what the Bible speaks about a certain topic. Perhaps some assignments will not be graded but necessary for a passing grade.

At each level, the student/disciple is learning many things. Let me briefly touch on one area.

Spiritual development is greatly aided through inner reflection, one of the spiritual disciplines. The individual needs to be quiet and hear what God is saying (even when busy with ministry, family or classes—or all three in some cases!). At each stage of spiritual development, this takes on different aspects.

(1) The new believer is learning to hear his or her Father's voice. The believer begins to be aware of the Holy Spirit working through the conscience and otherwise.

(2) The young believer learns to discern the Spirit's words in contrast to the evil one's words. This is the struggle lurking behind temptation. He or she will learn how to

---

[13] Christian parents often want something better than their children themselves want. This will complicate matters somewhat, but at least those attending will have extra motivation to be there.

properly respond to God's words and use them to protect him or herself and fight off temptation.

(3) The mature believer further develops what has been said, but focuses on enriching times of worship, being coached, guided, and protected by God, all being able to be used to pinpoint ways God wants to bear fruit through his or her life.

There are many aspects to this three-part development, but as a believer progresses through each, the growth is realized.

Fine tuning those goals and objectives

One's mental and physical maturity greatly shapes how fast a person can grow spiritually. Those who see others spiritually growing tend to grow quicker themselves. For example, if a believer near me gets excited about reading the Bible, then I get excited hearing him and want to replicate that in my own life.

Working with couples that will be getting married is a tremendous opportunity to lay a good foundation for their marriage. This is also an excellent time to train them on how to mentor other new couples, which can be added at the end of their training sessions if they are interested.

So let us go back to our earlier example. We could teach the engaged couple to combine the art of listening to God with their interest in forming a great marriage. We can help them learn how to listen to God and how relying on God helps one be a good husband or wife.

Or for those who are single, we can help them learn how one goes about finding the right wife or husband, or to understand what commitments are needed to become one. "What ways can God help me prepare to be a good husband?" Or as a potential wife, what are the principles of good communication for marriage? Overall we are training them to listen to God. Carefully listening to God greatly aids them in accomplishing their goal towards a great marriage.

Many things we learn are life-dependent; that is, we learn through our life experiences. Teaching a person who is not married how to be a good husband will have limited value. So combining our goal of listening to God along with an area of interest can further inspire them with the practicality of the subject.

Good mentors wanted

Godly mentors and teachers are critically needed, otherwise these students will not gain the faith they need and even worse, will be horribly polluted. If a teacher thinks porn and filthy movies are fine to watch, then spiritual adultery is in the making —even if the teacher is not blatant about it. The students will not gain faith for the beauty of a great marriage but learn from the teacher's mindset of a worldly marriage.

Here is how these principles might be briefly worked out through this life flow:

- God designs individuals responsibly listen to Him. They learn how to do this in each area of their lives.
- God intends to create beautiful marriages. We then can show them how spiritual disciplines and their intimacy with God have everything to do with having a great marriage. (Or singlehood as appropriate.)

We refrain from teaching merely an academic perspective of marriage, but instead instill the vision of a beautiful, godly marriage. We purpose that the students, no matter where they are in their own lives, work these things through with the clear goal of connecting these things to God's greater purposes and power.

Integration of The Life Core

We will spend only a little time discussing the integration of *The Life Core* into the overall training of Christian students. While it is hopeful that this eventually happens–as the major goal can more deeply penetrate each aspect of the organization, our focus here is on sharing the vision rather than techniques. We have hinted at how this might work out in the particular cases of listening to God and preparation for marriage, but there is much more to it and is best reserved for another time.

It takes time to instill vision, grapple with the implications of that vision in our churches or schools, understand the challenges of adopting God's goals, convincing others of the need for change, and the actual implementation of that vision. We must not be in a rush, and yet it needs to stand as a priority as we seek God's means of freshly adapt these concepts into our present programs and agenda. Many institutions have strong-minded boards that control funds and direction. Changes, then, become even more difficult to make. Some might say impossible. We start where we can and keep moving forward by God's leading. With more influence, we can do more. Someone wisely stated that it is easier to shape a new disciple than reshape an older believer. This is so true.

Preaching, communication, counseling courses, and other areas of learning in the educational environment will soon become powerful instruments when professors and students alike know how God will use *The Life Core* concepts to better enable them to teach and be like Christ. When the students begin to see the Spirit of God working in their lives and others through what they are learning, they will be all the more eager to learn.

Preaching will go beyond the actual sermon time to include classes on how to be changed and bring about changed hearts through the sermon. God and prayer becomes part of the training. We are now asking:

- What does God want me to preach on?

- How do I learn what He wants?

- How do I actually convey these things in the power of His Spirit?

- What place does prayer have in preaching?

Church history will be transformed from simply looking at what has transpired to an analysis of why the church was crippled or strengthened through certain events. This approach allows us to better see how having, or not having the truths of God acted out, affected the church at large and shaped people's heart in individual congregations.

Instead of just studying the Reformation we want to understand the context we now live in and how it is either similar or different. In this way, we will be able to discern what God wants to do and what our part in it is.

If the life core becomes completely integrated with other teaching, it could get lost and eventually buried. Other voices will clamor for attention, or traditions of men will take over. Whether the life core becomes integrated or holds a standalone path in our school, church, seminary, or family, however, we will be challenged to implement studies that aim at the target of spiritual transformation. In the following exercises we will give another opportunity to write out your chief goals.

Whether the life core program is integrated with other studies or not, the classes will need to be redeveloped somewhat to keep in step with the personal growth of the students.

A challenge

This book is only meant to be an introduction on how to restore godly training in schools, homes, and churches, first by introducing God's agenda and then provide different scenarios where God might lead you to take initiative. We are releasing the vision and are providing a few examples to push teachers and students, pastors and church members, to where they can and should be in God.

Generations of God's people have been cheated from the intimacy and power of God's truth. Things must change. Our purpose is to build up the full body of Christ into being a pure bride anticipating Christ's return. By establishing God's goals for us, we can then by faith, step by step, move closer to that goal.

As we identify the life core and what it looks like at different stages in one's spiritual development, then we can apply it to our particular situations. All at once, our potential as believers comes together with God's purposes and power for our lives. This is what we were chosen and designed for. Let's embrace it and start seeing how God will help us to reach that likeness of Christ here on earth.

Two general approaches

By keeping the life core training program separate from the main curriculum, it enables us to start small, use less financial resources, slowly pass on the vision, expand as godly mentors arise (to assure success), and make slow changes to the overall curriculum to more closely connect to the heart of godly training.

For example, though I am fully involved in this ministry of writing and international training, I am always prayerfully watching where I might find a few local people that needs to be mentored. Whether the church I am involved in has an active discipleship program or not, does not matter (fortunately it does). Find the right people and start mentoring. It is critical that we start with where we are and learn how the life core principles need to shape what we are doing. I have always tried to get other teachers to co-teach adult training classes with me. We take turns teaching but before teaching we meet together and discuss our lessons. These individuals later become teachers with the same vision and purpose. We have a heart not just for teaching The Book of Romans, for example but glorifying God by seeing the truths transform our lives.

To make a complete integration of the life core into our already established institutions is more consistent but requires bold leadership and risks opposition from those uncomfortable with upsetting the status quo. Along with the challenge to the teachers and pastors, we are also calling for a revolution of expectation from God's people to motivate slow and dull leaders across the globe to make godly changes.

Why should a seminarian give tens of thousands of dollars to an institution of higher learning for a degree that does not properly equip him or her? Why should a member attend a church that lacks the vision and faith for all of its members to grow up into Christ's image?

We need God-empowered implementation of the life core into our hearts, homes, churches, and training institutions to fully equip the church rather than enduring the increasing irrelevancy of the church. Why not instead be those bold leaders who insist on the proper implantation of the truth of God into our lives?

Lessons

- Integration of spiritual transformation into the lives of the students will require significant changes to the way schools and churches carry out their program and teaching.

- God's purposes as seen in the life core must be the chief focus for these churches and schools to see revival, to thrive and to flourish.

- Using the life core as a separate inner transformational track appears to be better than large scale changes, fully integrated into the whole program. Start small. Enjoy success. Widen the scope.

Memorize & Meditate

Philippians 2:14-16

Assignment

➡ Have you ever spiritually evaluated a person before? How so? What problems did you face?

➡ Define the life core. Do you agree this life core should be the central thrust of any Christian training? Explain.

➡ Evaluate the challenges that you might have making God's life core the central focus for your school, church, person, etc.?

#35 Leadership Development

Ministerial schools would no doubt state that they are all about developing good leaders in the particular fields for which their students are being trained: pastors, missionaries, counselors, administrators, teachers, etc. But are they?

I asked one pastor about his church's leadership training ministry. His denominational leaders wondered why he doesn't send them to their seminary and Bible school classes. He simply stated that the schools don't train his people for the work! Are those training in our best schools really being equipped with a strong faith to fight temptation, a developing love for God, adept in using God's Word as they compassionately serve others?

Spiritual growth and training

This book has focused on how to develop the basic foundation of godly leaders. Besides needing proper room to grow, they also need specific direction, depending on the individual's spiritual development. However, this fundamental training is meant and designed for all believers.

Without the cultivation of the spiritual life, a person cannot be a good leader. "For apart from me you can do nothing" (John 15:5). David the king had a similar thought: "Blessed be the LORD God, the God of Israel, who alone works wonders" (Psalm 72:18).

Spiritual growth is the elimination of those things that keep us away from and blinded to God's glorious presence. In a positive definition, spiritual development is adopting more of God's ways as one increases time and intimacy with God.

Secularism, materialism, and traditionalism are three pronounced forces in our modern world that distance us from Christ. The church does not need to live in fear of them unless she is not properly dressed with the armor of God.

The king with no clothes

Our models of learning often betray our real purposes. While a knowledgable command of the facts is important, this goal needs to be carefully placed on and around the life core principles so that information complements rather than hinders the development of one's spiritual life. Faith that issues from winning spiritual battles is what should bolster a Christian leader, not a bland mixture of self-esteem and self-confidence due to the accumulation of information.

Many Christian leaders and teachers, I fear, have never been properly trained to live their lives and ministries around Christ. For them, it is abstract rather than a reality. I have worked with many leaders across the globe. When presented with these discipleship training stages, most of them say to me that they have not even got out of stage two. They still wrestle to a great degree with various kinds of temptations.

When a leader falls, he is very susceptible to discouraging thoughts from the evil one. We all can fall but if it is common, then there is no faith to share with others about how they can live an overcoming life. Failure, thus, breeds more failure.

Allow me to share some of the ways I have found typical Christian training to be inadequate. We will analyze the weakness of leaders that stem from the lack of development at the first two stages of spiritual development.

Stage #1: The goal is to develop trust in God that comes from being secure in His love.

When leaders have never properly discovered God's constant love for their lives (supposed to be learned in stage 1), they tend to be very insecure about their own salvation and their views of ministry. Without a true understanding of the cross, the individual feels that he must strive to get God's acceptance through what he does. Ritualism, legalism, and overemphasis on one's own works replace true worship with worship of an idol.

Other problems can develop such as the tendency to seek an inordinate amount of attention from others, an inability to get beyond self to focus on properly loving and serving others.

Stage #2: The goal is to learn to use God's Word to overcome temptation.

Without a clear growth of trust from stage #1, the believer cannot easily go beyond stage #2. Most experiences of Christian life will be lived in a sphere of dismal failure.

The young believer is to have strong confidence in God's Word, right? But what happens when he or she discovers that temptation cannot overcome? Such a believer becomes convinced that the Word is irrelevant to them. God takes a backseat in terms of how they live daily and try to grow spiritually.

This attitude will stain their overall concepts of ministry and God's Word. Instead of breeding confidence in God's Word, the evil one will insidiously insert doubts into their minds leading to deeper problems:

(1) Permitting sin in their lives

(2) Tolerating religious living rather than the cultivation of intimacy with God

(3) Acceptance of inferior concepts of God's Word

(4) Belief that specialists are needed to help with deeper spiritual struggles because they cannot handle them on their own

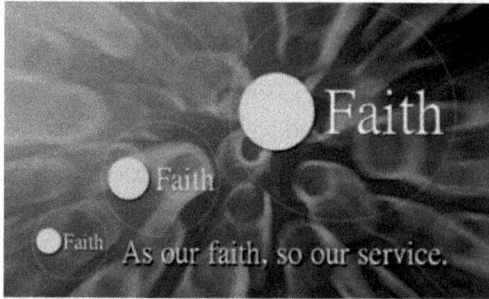

Faith

Faith

Faith As our faith, so our service.

Understanding genuine ministry

If our greatest ministry comes from intimacy with Christ, then we must admit that when we tolerate unholy aspects of our lives, no matter how much we struggle with them, this lack of intimacy with God will compromise our effectiveness. Our ministry, then, becomes focused on our own experience, skills, and opportunities rather than a joint ministry between the Lord and us.

Any minister or teacher's sin is bound to become a key weakness that the evil one will exploit, not only to destroy that person but to weaken his or her ministry.

This is but a brief glance at the reasons we need godly leaders. Many have succumbed to their lusts, been attracted by the world's idea of success, built up their own self-image or stored up bitterness in their hearts. The glorious gospel love is not at all shown through their lives. They are not able to grow, and the life that is in them is diminished.

The church and Christian ministry schools must realize that urgent breakthroughs in training are needed to restore God's people to the glorious position God has called them.

And those who have insight will shine brightly like the brightness of the expanse of heaven, and those who lead the many to righteousness, like the stars forever and ever (Daniel 12:3).

Godly leaders by definition must come from stage three of Christian growth. They can still greatly benefit through training, knowledge, and skill development, but godly character remains fundamental for effective Christian service for it gauges the degree of intimacy with God.

Godly leadership

One exciting aspect of this study is God's willingness to get intimately involved in the process of training leaders. The very life that He has put in our hearts strives by its gospel DNA to grow up into Christ's image.[14]

Note the way Paul has described the various aspects of godly leadership in an overseer. His life needs to be fully interwoven with his leadership position.

If any man be above reproach, the husband of one wife, having children who believe, not accused of dissipation or rebellion. For the overseer must be above reproach as God's steward, not self-willed, not quick-tempered, not addicted to wine, not pugnacious, not fond of sordid gain, but hospitable, loving what is good, sensible, just, devout, self-controlled, holding fast the faithful word which is in accordance with the teaching, that he may be able both to exhort in sound doctrine and to refute those who contradict (Titus 1:6-9).

---

[14] DNA refers to the self-replicating and purposed molecular chains that enable our physical bodies to grow and develop.

This is not just a list of qualities that the society considered important in the culture at that place and time. Much more is being stated. The integrity with which we live out our personal lives in light of God's holy purposes directly influences how we influence and train people.

One of our books, *The Godly Man*[15], expands on the idea that true godliness comes from being close to God. We use ten different character traits of God, showing how they influence a man's life.

The need for godliness

Confidence that derives from God's holy work within us produces a trust that enables us:

(1) To live close to God

(2) To persevere when tried

(3) To effectively minister God's Word to others.

Without this confidence, it is best that we do not minister. Or even better, we learn how to gain that confidence and continue on in our ministry. With the right heart and faith, improvements can rapidly take place.

God desires to raise godly leaders and dislikes our attempts to produce leaders without this godly character. We unleash God's power in our training and the church at large by seeking the development of what is important in a leader. They need a heart that seeks after God, whether it's through our personal lives, ministries, or training of others.

But the LORD said to Samuel, "Do not look at his appearance or at the height of his stature, because I have rejected him; for God sees not as man sees, for man looks at the outward appearance, but the LORD looks at the heart" (1 Samuel 16:7).

---

[15] *The Godly Man: When God Touches a Man's Life:*
www.foundationsforfreedom.net/Help/Store/Intros/
Godly_Man_intro.html

If our churches and schools could make sure this basic training was instilled in its people, surely the Word of God would mightily grow in our midst for godly leaders would enable God's Spirit to powerfully move among His people.

Lessons

- We must become impatient and non-tolerant of training schemes that don't insist on life transformation that is so necessary for godly leadership and training.
- Our standards must include godly living, otherwise the acceptable standard becomes loathsome in God's eyes and everyone suffers.
- God has a special way of restoring all believers and bringing them to godly living so that they can be eligible for godly leadership.

Memorize & Meditate

Titus 1:5-9

Assignment

➡ Are you a Christian leader? Are you godly? Explain.

➡ Do you know of any ungodly leaders in any church, Christian school, or ministry? If so, identify some of the problems that ensue.

➡ If you attended a ministry school, did they train the heart attitude, and conduct? Was it voluntary? How did it work out? How could it be improved?

▸ Life in the Spirit! describes the Holy Spirit's way of working in our lives from before conversion to being fully used by Him.

#36 Training in Churches

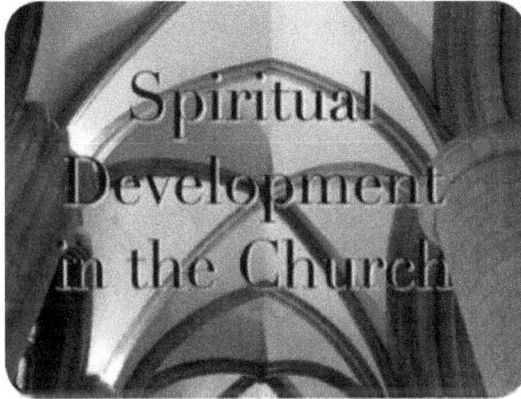

The local church and even entire denominations need to focus on the training of their leaders because the leaders shape the church. As the pastors live and preach, so the people of God go.[16]

The influence of leaders

The books of Judges and Kings give us plenty of examples portraying different kinds of leaders. Brave leaders like Gideon and King David are contrasted with poor leaders like Samson and King Ahab with his wife Jezebel. There are differences of titles and expectations between these judges and kings of the past with today's pastors, teachers, and elders. But, no matter what generation, the influence of leaders on the people of God cannot be denied.

---

[16] The opposite can be true too, as the people are, so are the leaders. When appointed leaders no longer act as true leaders, they are just an expression of an ungodly society.

No local church should expect to go beyond where their pastor is spiritually. The same is true with a family or school. Is this not what Jesus meant by saying, "A disciple is not above his teacher, nor a slave above his master" (Matthew 10:24)?

There are major forces countering a biblical faith which produce what we see as a 'natural' tendency towards drifting into unbelief and less integrity. Civilizations, similarly, tend to go from strong to weak.

The Spirit of God is present and actively working,[17] but when the leaders tolerate compromise in their lives, the Spirit is restrained from working. The people of God begin to imitate or at least tolerate the pastor's attitudes toward worldliness, religious pretense, and immorality.

The Lord is not bound to work only through the leaders, but these leaders have a great influence on the spiritual health of the church. The best place to train them is in the churches first and then the seminaries.

Trying hard

But what if you do have a pastor that is keen on spiritually developing the people of God? How does this work out in the congregation? Pastors tell me, "I tried this or that method, but do not know what to do next"

The greatest problem facing such churches is that there is no overall map. The church's general goals are good ones worthy of pursuit, but they have no way to bring God's people to that point.

They see a certain need here and there, and they do their best to address it. But more often than not, these efforts serve more as a patch than a solution. They are temporary and reveal

---

[17] The dynamics in churches where the Spirit has left from His active work needs to be more fully explored (Revelation 2-3).

that the underlying issues are deeper than the one or two easily seen problems.

God's greater work

Without embracing God's greater work, we often become focused on patching rather than major repairs. God has a great goal for the church here on earth. The local church is a living and dynamic group of people through which God greatly desires to work and display His glory.

Having been built upon the foundation of the apostles and prophets, Christ Jesus Himself being the corner stone, in whom the whole building, being fitted together is growing into a holy temple in the Lord; in whom you also are being built together into a dwelling of God in the Spirit (Ephesians 2:20-22).

The church's distinction

In the following chapter we will highlight the difference that the life core can make on a Christian training institution. Much of what applies to the local church scene is applicable to other Christian training institutions.

The church, however, is distinctive from training institutions in several ways. The church does not merely train the people of God, it is the people of God. Organizationally speaking, there are yet other differences. For example, the workers are largely not being paid; they are volunteers. Church members typically remain in a local church longer than in a school where they might attend for only several years.

Lastly, church teachers usually have less frequent teaching opportunities than in a seminary or Bible college. For example, though a professor might only have one class a week with the student, he or she can require the reading of books and writing of papers throughout the week. A pastor or Sunday School class teacher can rarely can get away with this!

Let me discuss these differences one by one.

Extended contact and personal mentoring

Time is a crucial factor. The church benefits are seen in the way it allows us to gain a deeper involvement in the lives of the individuals. On the other hand, too much time can cause us to lose focus. Nothing seems urgent–except the crisis counseling case. Church, class, or program attendance often becomes confused with spiritual development.

Schools are focused on what has to happen semester by semester. The church, on the other hand, tends to assume all will work out fine if the people just faithfully attend the service and given Sunday School classes. There is little sense of purpose except to continue to attend and give.

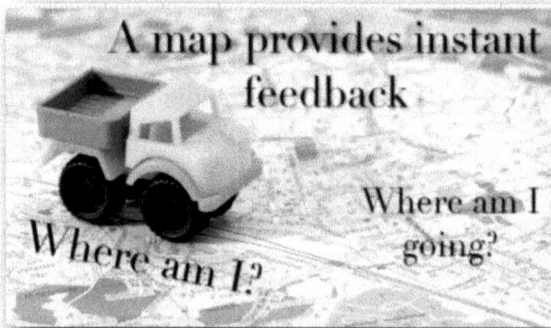

A map provides instant feedback

Where am I?

Where am I going?

A spiritual map is important!

The life core helps us to map out a life development chart along with the opportunity to serve and bear fruit. Church leaders, like kind shepherds, meet individually with each member and help them discern which discipleship level they are at. They can also identify where his or her foundation might be a bit shaky. Personal relationships and time spent together allows us to mentor these individuals without disturbing class deadlines about what's next on the agenda.

In a church, even if a person is getting married, he or she will be back after the honeymoon. Training can continue upon their return. (Or even better, we can train them for a good marriage!) Time is on our side.

Church leaders can have helpful discussions identifying ways to develop these shaky foundations and move these folks ahead in their spiritual development with the goal of eventually effectively serving others.

Less direct influence

In contrast to a professor, the pastor rarely has opportunity to teach on a deeper theological level. Because the time is limited, every hour counts. The strength of the church is its ability to powerfully proclaim God's Word and create a niche for God's Word to take root. The Bible allows, if not demands, that we keep focused on the major themes of salvation, sanctification, and outreach.

A problem, however, can and does occur when the people themselves are not growing. A church's clear vision might increase motivation but not necessarily spiritual growth and maturity. What is this dullness that makes God's people unable to respond to good preaching and teaching?

There are many contributing factors including our own sin! John in Revelation 2-3 identifies many of these areas that cause lukewarmness, but, we also see John again and again pointing back to restoration.

In each of the addresses to the seven churches, John begins by referring to Jesus' rightful place in the church, each being pertinent to the need at hand. For Smryna, Jesus was the resurrected one. The fear of death should not hold back the church (Revelation 2:8-11). For Pergamum, the sharp two-edged sword assures of sure judgment of wickedness in the church (Revelation 2:12-17). And so on. Restoration will always bring our focus back to the glorious place Christ Jesus has in our lives

Restoration is the reconnection of a person's life plans back to the center focus of life, the Lord. As the believer gains a better feel of direction from the spiritual map (i.e., three levels of discipleship), their eagerness to grow is often restored. When the overall goal is combined with special tasks that the mentor provides, they gain a sense of confidence that they can reach that goal and are more willing to participate.

The pastor should be easily able to develop an overall vision of what God is doing in the lives of the flock of God. If this is combined with a carefully developed mentoring program, then the people of God will increase in excitement, not chiefly from the church, but from their Lord and His work in them.

Less motivated

God's people cannot be made to go to class. They have not contributed tens of thousands of dollars so that they will get a degree. If church training is properly conducted, however, people will personally see God transforming their lives and will respond in delight and worship. People no longer 'have' to be there but want to be there. Others are motivated to attend by those that are excited about what God is doing in their lives

This is the picture of the church of God, God dwelling in His people's midst. Personal transformation must take place along with public preaching and teaching if God is to live in their midst. When we tolerate the lack of personal holiness and spiritual growth, then we will no longer welcome God and His work in our midst. "In whom you also are being built together into a dwelling of God in the Spirit" (Ephesians 2:22).

Summary

The local church is a great place for training and need not fear that it cannot compete with the seminary. It can if it does its job properly! The reason many go to seminary is to find this purpose and counsel which they could not find in their local church.

This trend to take more courses outside the church is good in some ways. And yet, I wonder if it also does not reveal the lack of proper training and opportunities for service in the church. When pastors are continually growing in their spiritual love for the Lord and others, it is infectious. The people will do the same. They will be eager to grow and serve others more.[18]

The church must be much more diligent in helping believers grow strong and should not just expect it will happen 'naturally'.

Lessons

- The church has a great opportunity and obligation to clarify where each believer is in his or her spiritual growth, how to work through problems, and to lead him or her on to fruitful service.

- The people of God are very interested to know God's will for their lives and how it is to be implemented. Address these issues in a biblical context and the people of God will become engaged.

- God greatly desires to build the people of God up as His holy temple. He is seeking those leaders that will work along with Him to bring glory to God through presenting a godly people to Him for service. By helping individuals grow, the church is making the greatest contribution to developing strong leaders for themselves and other churches.

Memorize & Meditate

Ephesians 2:21-22

---

[18] There are at times authority-grabbing church elders work against the pastor to preserve their own interests. This goes beyond the discussion here.

Assignment

➡ Describe the church that you now attend in light of the things stated above. Are the people excited about growing? Why or why not?

➡ Do church leaders mentor the members in such a way they know where they are in their spiritual growth and how to reach the next step?

➡ Are the people maturing and naturally serving others

➡ What percentage of the people take part in the care and building up of the church (including administration and facility operations)?

▸ *Fostering Spiritual Growth in the Church* found in the Discipleship #1 Digital Library further elaborates on what happens at each stage of spiritual development.

#37 Integration in Training Schools

In this chapter we will focus on how training in Christian collegiate schools as well as ministerial training schools can benefit from keeping this life source in mind. Schools are a more regulated environment than churches. Courses must fit into an overall curriculum.

However, if one's purpose is build solid and secure, spiritual lives, life training at the core level must take place. These essential life building blocks are connected to every other area of training. Let me provide an example.

One lovely couple

A young couple, along with their two children, came to pastor a congregation. They had just graduated from a great seminary and looked like a wonderful fit. They were outgoing and eager to get involved in this new pastoring situation. Several years later, however, it was discovered they suffered from severe marital conflict. They couldn't get along with each other. This tension also manifested itself in the husband's somewhat arrogant form of leadership. The sad ending is quite predictable. Only later did we discover that these marital problems were ongoing even during seminary training.

Though the seminary offered good training, their poor marriage meant that the foundation for a ministry was not there. These kinds of problems are increasing all the time as the number of dysfunctional families increase in our society.

Getting back to our goals

The man graduated from seminary but yet his life was in shambles. What is the goal of seminaries or those schools preparing people for ministry? Should they graduate those who have personal or marital struggles? To some, these questions are preposterous. How could they not graduate them?

Churches, however, assume those that graduate from these seminaries have grown in maturity because they passed their allotted courses. And yet, the schools are not providing the character and spiritual maturity training these individuals need. This is precisely why merely passing on knowledge and handing out certificates does not achieve the goal of spiritual maturity.

We must subject the educational methodologies of our schools to the greater purpose of the Lord to further refine our training. If the goal is to prepare people for ministry, then we must adequately shape them for that ministry. Training must go beyond supplying knowledge to the purposeful shaping of their attitudes and commitment to serving.

Few will challenge this need as it is fundamental to the Gospel. We are to love one another. Our lives are seized by God to live out His purposes of passing genuine care on to others.

For you were called to freedom, brethren; only do not turn your freedom into an opportunity for the flesh, but through love serve one another (Galatians 5:13).

Although we want the best, it is easy to become cynical when, year after year, these goals are not being fulfilled. The need becomes an extraordinary problem if your church receives one of these unequipped pastors.

A better way

The Life Core (along with the life process analogy) clarifies how to face these challenges. By using God's life goals to shape the central core goals for training, a school can gain a fully integrated framework that is designed to grow the entire person, intellectual as well as spiritual. Inherent to this comprehensive approach is the ability to observe different segments of growth, the goals, and processes that occur during certain periods of spiritual development.

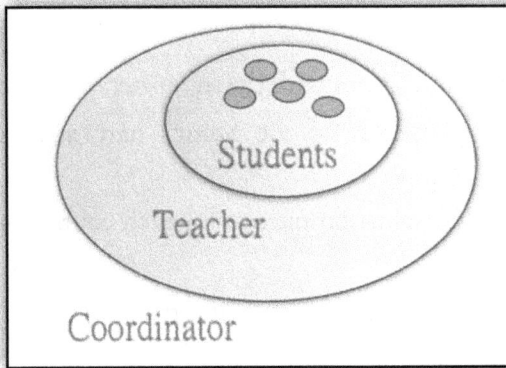

This approach enables instructors to create courses, training opportunities, and specialized projects to aid in their students' development. Suggestions on how to make the life core the central focus of training will come later in another chapter. Here, however, we will see what this comprehensive perspective can do for the coordinator, teacher, and student.

Christian schools often utilize selective items listed below, but if they are not well coordinated, or form only parts rather than the whole, they will not experience the full power that God wants to bring into the scene. For clarity, we have analyzed this from three points of view: the principal (coordinator), teacher, and student.

Coordinator's Responsibilities (e.g. Principal or Planning Committee)

- Assure a unified core integrates all the training.
- Provide confidence that training is reaching the hearts of the students.
- Focus on accomplishing God's purposes for God's glory.
- Aim at a goal that everyone can identify with, administration, teacher, and student.
- Openly recognize that everyone is on the same page of growth, including teachers, administration, and students.
- Clearly affirm that God's goal of serving is best and necessary.
- Provide transparency with the supporters of the school.
- Increase awareness of the Spirit's part and purpose in training.
- Clarify the evaluation process for each course and training experience.
- Integrate spiritual life with course training.

Teacher's and Trainer's Responsibilities

- Take each course and see its place within the whole.
- Openly discuss the way the courses connect to the students' spiritual development and service.
- Find increased meaning and excitement in academic teaching.
- Seek God's involvement in the course as a whole as well as for each class.

- Receive encouragement seeing how God is using him or her to properly equip others.
- Keep God as part of the teaching process.
- Embrace God's higher goal and seek God to accomplish these goals.
- Seek God's special wisdom to properly teach the students.
- Communicate this vision to learners.
- Reveal the power of God's truth as he equips students facing incredible personal problems.
- Confidently point students to rely on God to find solutions rather than those outside the church.
- Believe students are being cared for personally as well as intellectually.

Student's Responsibilities

- Understand God's overall preparation for his or her life so as to carry out His purpose.
- Recognize how this formal training is related to God's purpose in his life and ministry.
- See how the training further enables him or her to accomplish God's greater goals in and through his life.
- Evaluate where he or she is in his or her spiritual life path.
- Be stirred on towards further growth and thus lessen the temptation toward pride.
- Be encouraged by past growth.
- Regularly remind him or herself that the training is integrated with his or her whole life.
- Sense God's personal care for his or her whole life.
- Gain an integrated picture of how the skill and knowledge training is connected to his or her spiritual foundation.
- Be enriched by discovering solutions for existing unsolvable personal struggles.
- Be set free from sin! Grow in faith.

- Focus on service.
- Overcome discouragement from past failures.
- Learn to train others no matter their stage of spiritual development.

This is a win–win situation for all.

These goals bring the students into greater conformity with God's overall purpose for the church, so that as the church becomes more like Christ, His glory shines brighter and greater here on earth.

A Separate Curriculum

By having a separate life core development in addition to one's regular curriculum, these things might be better addressed in a way that guides the student to profit most from his or her experiences. Any student going into ministry will not only be personally tested but also will want to be used to help others regain their passion, more deeply commit their lives to the Lord, and to stimulate believers into yet further growth.

There will be difficulties that arise in schools. How is one to intertwine the life core with the regular curriculum? What happens if we find those people are unwilling to grow? Or what can we say to those who face very difficult problems?

This is not the place to work through all the details. In the end, a school or church must keep the larger life goals in mind while carrying out its services. If, however, our services are not reaching our goals, then we need to prayerfully rethink through the process.

Lessons

- Coordinators gain increased confidence to integrate the necessary training to provide genuine preparation for ministry.
- Teachers find increased meaning in teaching by further discovering how their training is part of the student's full development.

- Students learn to overcome sin and train others to grow in Christ no matter where they are in their spiritual development.

Memorize & Meditate

Galatians 5:13

Assignment

➡ State your experiences as a past or current student. What is your level of spiritual growth? Do you think that training, secular or otherwise, has helped you serve others in the full power of the Holy Spirit? Explain.

➡ Have you trained or taught others? Did you encounter problems with integrating a subject with your student's spiritual needs or God's life goals for them? Explain.

➡ How did Paul summarize his life purpose in Acts 27:23? Why are each of these elements so important for living our lives to our fullest?

"For this very night an angel of the God to whom I belong and whom I serve stood before me" (Acts 27:23).

➡ If you are a Christian college teacher or administrator, do you find that your school embraces this life core purpose? Explain. What difficulties might arise if you further implemented it?

#38 Training in Christian K-12 Schools

Christian schools train many children. More than one and a quarter million annually attend American Protestant schools.[19] While secular education is getting more secularistic, immoral, and outright vulgar in its activities, an increasing number of parents are turning to Christian schools and home schools for refuge. What damage secularization is bringing to our children! This is one of the outcomes of idolizing knowledge over character and relationship with God.

Schools are important!

The training Christian schools provide is invaluable, especially considering the hours they have with the children, but let it not be forgotten that the vision and place of mentoring should primarily be done in the church and family. However, hardly

---

[19] 25% of total of 5,488,000 in 2010-2011. http://www.capenet.org/facts.html

any churches are discipling their people. Families can always use good support. (They could work with other families who are modeling this type of training to accomplish this.)

Can the Christian schools utilize these discipleship concepts and training tools? Absolutely. The most important part is starting with the right mentors. Once we have identified God's primary way of working, we would be foolish not to actively promote His program. Just because some might neglect their responsibilities, this does not mean we should stand at their side and let them perish. This has become an opportunity to bring about a more complete training regimen.

Transform not merely educate

Think about God's desires for these schools and children:

- Children who zealously seek God's purpose for their lives.

- Children who are motivated by God's love for others.

- Children who are convinced God's ways and purposes are even greater than that which so powerfully allures them in this world.

The world can only seem powerful when the power of the Word of God appears irrelevant. The best weaponry is to bare God's glorious purposes and power to His people.

That He would grant you, according to the riches of His glory, to be strengthened with power through His Spirit in the inner man; so that Christ may dwell in your hearts through faith; and that you, being rooted and grounded in love, may be able to comprehend with all the saints what is the breadth and length and height and depth, and to know the love of Christ which surpasses knowledge, that you may be filled up to all the fulness of God (Ephesians 3:16-19).

Challenges with implementation

God's goals allow us to be honest in our goals, clear in our approach, and creative in our methodology. Challenges often arise when instituting changes. This is what leaders are made for!

Look carefully at your school's goals. Are they being fulfilled? Tally up the shortcomings. This list can often be used to fortify one's reasons to request or implement changes. Schools should not ignore, or even worse, despise churches and parents that seek a more character-centric education for their children, but they should consider them as partners assisting the school to accomplish its goals.

There are certain cautions, however. The greatest problem is working with unbelievers. While the church as a whole confesses belief, many students do not. While God does want and demand holiness in each teacher and child, not every one has the Holy Spirit working in his or her life. Many have no heart for the things of God, they simply want the relative benefits of a Christian school over a secular school.

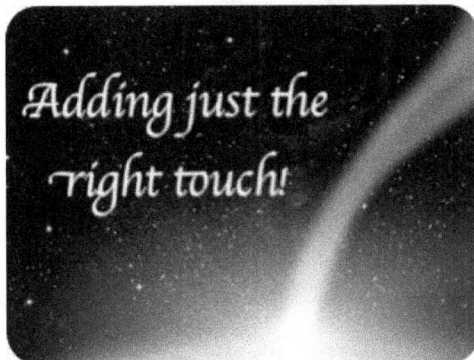

Adding just the right touch!

Superficial confessions of faith are no substitute for genuine Spirit-worked regeneration. No interest indicates the lack of God's work in their hearts. Nor should we pretend all the students are the 'children of God.' These children first need to be saved before God can dynamically work in their lives.

The same problem exists in the home. While we hope and pray that all our children know the Lord, not all do. We still train, however, with the hope that they will come to know the Lord. Without Jesus, however, there is no spiritual life and therefore no spiritual growth. At home, we can adopt various styles of training, taking into account these matters. With schools, it is more difficult.

Perhaps, a better approach is to treat this training, or parts of it, as elective rather than mandatory for all children. Focus on providing mentoring for those who are interested, parent or child.

The school has a lot of advantages with both time and continuity of relationship. Furthermore, the students often have extra time (due to school-provided "extended day care," for instance) to focus on these important areas of development.

Finding qualified mentors

Budget problems will always exist, but the largest problem is staffing–finding qualified mentors. There are few people that are properly trained or sufficiently mature to conduct such mentoring. I sense, however, with some good coaching, there are many that would love to help the students spiritually thrive.

If the school is closely associated with a church, which is often the case, the church could challenge and equip some of its own members to help in this area, either by volunteering or receiving pay. Children, once trained, can serve as mentors to other children in some basic ways. Be open to how God can work in surprising ways through the lives of children.

Effective training in schools

If qualified leaders can gain the vision and tools of training children, then this provides the framework for a good training program. Selective curriculum and Bible studies complemented with individual mentoring provides the best environment for spiritual development.

Be cautious regarding the use of charts purporting to measure spiritual development in children. For example, the time span in which a regular adult believer can grow is often much quicker than a child. The three to four months a new believer typically needs can expand to three to four years in children, depending on the age and situation. A curriculum needs to be adjusted with these facts in mind. Several different charts might need to be utilized for specialized situations to keep everyone accurately focused on God's goals in the children.

The school would be wise to engage its young people in special ways as their minds begin to mature and as they move through puberty. There will be special challenges and questions that need to be addressed to continue to show the relevance of the life core to their lives.

Explaining the mental and physical changes happening to them can help them realize the importance of nurturing their spiritual lives during this time. Even if they completed the second stage training (i.e., "young men"), it might be best to go through it again with special application and emphasis on their new sets of problems and spiritual battles at a different phase of physical and emotional development.

The increased amount of time available in schools is very helpful for specialized training, taking into consideration special problems and situations that are faced. For example, as they approach the end of their education, they could study career choice, mate choice, etc., with the whole purpose of God in mind.

The challenge is to go beyond Bible knowledge. The Bible needs to be taught with a purpose. The children need to see how it applies to living fulfilling lives in Christ.

All Scripture is inspired by God and profitable for teaching, for reproof, for correction, for training in righteousness; that the man of God may be adequate, equipped for every good work (2 Timothy 3:16-17).

Unless we can bind these truths to their lives, then they will look at these truths as irrelevant, "out there," and easy to toss away. If we can show them the relevancy of God's Word to their lives, however, a strong generation of young believers will develop.

Be aware of pride

There is always danger of pride, even in the heart of true biblical training and worship. Due to their immaturity, children are especially susceptible. With proper training, however, the child (and adult alike) can shake off temptations to be haughty by focusing on the joy of humbling serving others. This will frustrate the devil's attempt to hold back spiritual development. Children respect genuine spiritual development they see in others.

Summary

Christian schools can offer awesome spiritual training opportunities. Class training along with good mentors create great training times. By presenting a constant image of what God desires combined with significant moments to affirm these choices, children can more easily identify and accept God's values while rejecting the evil found in the world.

Lessons

K-12 Christian schools have a wonderful opportunity to train up believers due to their ongoing contact with them. The biggest challenges for these schools are:

- Knowing how to handle unbelieving students.
- Developing training material for the young who mature more slowly due to their age.

- Gaining transformed mentors equipped with the Life Core vision.

- Properly relating to parents, churches and authorities.

Memorize & Meditate

2 Timothy 3:16-17

Ephesians 3:16-19

Assignment

➡ Have you ever been to a Christian school or home school? What was the spiritual training like? Was it sufficient? Explain.

➡ Would these schools be competing with the churches if they provided in-depth mentoring? Explain.

➡ Do you have any experience dealing with unbelieving children in a church or school? How do you handle them? What more could be done?

➡ Are you a K-12 school administrator or teacher? Consider some of the challenges to implement these changes. Explain each. Start praying!

#39 A Long Term Perspective

Just as the Lord designed our bodies to physically grow and develop, He also arranged for His people to grow spiritually. The Lord provides each believer a unique set of interests and giftings which direct that individual to his or her God-given potential.

While we have presented many challenges, if we stop with what has been presented so far, our perspective would end up being somewhat distorted. There is yet another stage beyond the three we have discussed, one that we need spiritual insight to embrace.

Looking beyond

In the age to come, God will transform our bodies and present us to Himself whole and complete, with new bodies. This will continue on into eternity. For those who persevere, there is a crown of life:

Blessed is a man who perseveres under trial; for once he has been approved, he will receive the crown of life which the Lord has promised to those who love Him (James 1:12).

One characteristic of life is to aspire for continuity, to live as long as possible and to perpetuate its existence by reproduction. Although some teach that death is normal, it is untrue. If death was just another part of life, then funerals would not be the grief-filled events that they are.

Our spiritual lives reach their fulfillment and culmination when we stand as a perfect and complete entity before God in His presence. Jesus warns His followers not to think that what we see on earth is all there is to life. Life transcends our experience on earth.

Living by faith not only means understanding God's will on earth, but to rightly prioritize what we do to complete His will with the short time given to us. This only comes when we live in light of eternity. Then we can begin to rightly proportion our time and focus our energies on earth.

Long-term training

Our concept of eternity greatly shapes not only how we perceive our time on earth but how we train others. Without this overlying perspective of time running out and eternity moving in, our priorities will always be askew. I love how John puts it:

*Beloved, now we are children of God, and it has not appeared as yet what we will be. We know that when He appears, we will be like Him, because we will see Him just as He is. **And everyone who has this hope fixed on Him purifies himself**, just as He is pure (1 John 3:2-3).*[20]

Notice how this hope of what will be can further spur on our spiritual development, especially in the area of purity (but

---

[20] This is my favorite Bible verse!

that also shapes our fruit). The clearer our perspective of the truth, the more we will be shaped by it.

Seeking for God's city

Stage #3 speaks about maturity, but that is not our end goal. It is merely a holding pattern while on earth. Along with the creation which moans and groans under its present restraints (Romans 8:18-22), so we too long to be clothed with the garments of righteousness and live in the Lord's presence, apart from sin's poisonous touch.

And not only this, but we ourselves, having the first fruits of the Spirit, even we ourselves groan within ourselves, waiting eagerly for our adoption as sons, the redemption of our body (Romans 8:23).

This future transformation keeps us alert as to what is most important on earth. The whole analogy of life is transformed by the truth of the resurrection. Life is not just what we experience here on earth but to be shaped by what will be. That greater hope overshadows our present activities and dreams.

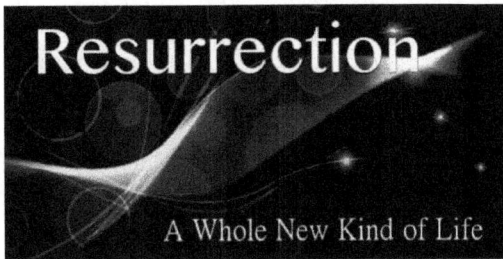

Every believer should be thoroughly excited at the prospects of what God now wants to do in his or her life here on earth in light of our coming transformation. Compared to the immensity of the future promises of God, the changes here are minimal, though still significant. We cannot, we dare not, however, minimize our spiritual life and development on earth.

Without new life, there is no eternal life. Without joining God's family, we cannot forever be a member of his family.

Accountability for our training

God has made it so that our earthly spiritual development and the bearing of fruit here on earth will be accordingly rewarded in the future. This is the measure by which believers will be judged when this life is over. He will discern our efforts and devotion. God will compare what we could have done with what we actually did.

Jesus in a parable reminding us of God's expectations closes by rebuking the man that saved his one talent, "But his master answered and said to him, 'You wicked, lazy slave, you knew that I reap where I did not sow, and gather where I scattered no seed'" (Matthew 25:26).

Paul uses this image of planting seed and growth in 1 Corinthians 3, "But each will receive his own reward according to his own labor" (1 Corinthians 3:8). God will examine the quality of our work according to His standard, not ours.

Each man's work will become evident; for the day will show it because it is to be revealed with fire, and the fire itself will test the quality of each ma's work. If any man's work which he has built on it remains, he will receive a reward. If any man's work is burned up, he will suffer loss; but he himself will be saved, yet so as through fire (1 Corinthians 3:13-15).

God has revealed many secrets about spiritual matters as well as future things. There is no doubt of the many, yet unrevealed, aspects of the fullness and glory of the life that we will inherit. He hints at them and assures us of their full unveiling in an age yet to come (Mark 10:29-30; Romans 8:21). These truths provide extra motivation for us to align our lives— all that we do and say—in light of these eternal truths.

Life becomes, after all, not just something God is causing to happen to us, but our own responses to what God has given to us. We have a great impact on what will happen to us in eternity by what we do here on earth and with what spirit we do it. This brief present life of ours shapes our eternal futures.

At times we sit down with our children and look at old pictures or videos. They capture scenes from the past which elicit memories of past decisions. We chose to live in a foreign country for the span of ten years. My wife and I also decided to homeschool our children. These decisions are reflected in our later lives and photos, as well as in the shaping of those we have had influence upon. Eternity will be similar. The connection of our eternal lives will be related to what we have done here in time.

Our opportunity

Our purpose here in this chapter is to remind us that there are greater goals for our lives than growth for growth's sake. We are to bear fruit which impacts the lives around us. The fruit that originates from intimacy with Christ not only ushers God's love and light into our world but shapes how God will treat us in eternity.

The best way to view life, perhaps, is a series of opportunities to respond to the One that grants us physical and spiritual life.

We seek effective godly training, not only because of promised rewards, which is obviously a motivation, but the joy we experience seeing those around us succeed. We desire that they, like us, might catch a glimpse of God's glorious light and life, be changed, grow into Christ's fullness, bear lasting fruit (John 15:16), and wonderfully enjoy their earthly spiritual development in eternity with the Lord and us.

Jesus said it, we do it

Jesus, holding all authority in heaven and earth, simply told us to make disciples because there is no greater good than to train others to know and love God. This has great benefits for our own lives as well. This is exactly what Jesus did (Isaiah 53:10-12) and what He calls His disciples to do. Making disciples is all important to our lives, to the welfare of those around us, and directly affects the glory of God revealed on earth.

Why is it then that so few make disciples? Why are we so fascinated with degrees, knowledge, attendance, etc., and so little engage in this concept of life transformation? Our lack of experiencing God's power in our own lives has everything to do with how seldom we seek for life transformation in those around us.

Lessons

- Although there are three stages of spiritual development on earth, that is not the end. We will experience a resurrection into a greater and more glorious eternal stage, just as Jesus did.
- We will be fully rewarded in the coming age according to our life and labor in this one. The consequences of not training godliness into the people of God will be tragic.
- We engage in training because we delight to see God's people growing into their fullness and through their growth able to bear much fruit that remains.

Memorize & Meditate

1 John 3:2-3

James 1:12

Assignment

➡ How much does eternity influence your own motivation and devotion to serving the Lord?

➡ Meditate on Matthew 28:18-20. Do you think Jesus is waiting for us to disciple so that He can unleash more of His power on earth? How is His authority connected to His command?

➡ Do you chiefly think about your own growth or the growth of others? Explain what degree of your motivation and joy comes from seeing the success of others.

#40 The Life Force

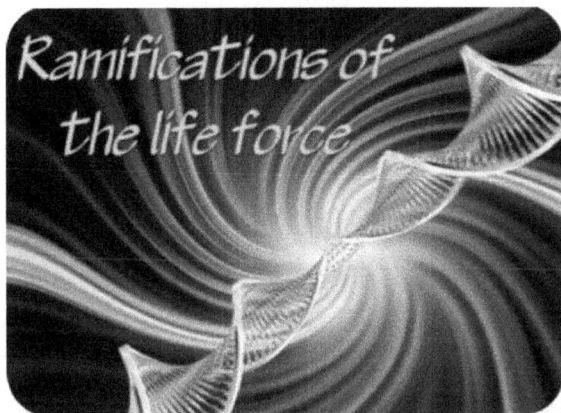

Ramifications of the life force

Our challenge in this book was to make that which is unobservable but real to be so vivid that it constantly influences the way we approach our lives, especially with regard to our training.

More than a process

We are not just observing a process in a clinical manner the way a biologist would. A biologist can only watch his experiments. We are called to experience the life God, not just research it.

Perhaps, we too, have committed grave error as theologians, pastors, teachers, and Christian leaders. We have focused on our service but have given little attention to Christ's empowering life within us and others.

Penetrating questions for the trainer

The Life Core has repeatedly focused on a few important questions:

➡ "Are we properly equipping others for ministry and service?"

➡ "Have we carefully evaluated what makes for trained leaders?"

➡ "Why is it that we tolerate substandard character traits that ruin any hope of godly leadership?"

No matter what institution we belong to or what local church we serve in, or even what position we bear, what matters is that we are discipling others so that they experience life transformation. (I use discipling in a broad manner here to include preaching, teaching, counseling, home visiting, mentoring, interviews, purposed conversations that focus on life transformation. One-to-one discipleship is one of the most effective places to make this happen.)

If what we do does not produce this life change, then we urgently need to recalculate what and how we do things, whether it be in our lives or others. We might pride ourselves in our schools, churches, and numbers, but without people reflecting Christ's image and replicating Christ's love and light in others, our labor is in vain.

Taking up the charge

Our challenge is to equip others so that they can and will disciple other people at the three different stages of spiritual growth. Each believer goes through these stages and so by not reinventing the wheel, we participate in God's effective methodology for growth.

"And we proclaim Him, admonishing every
man and teaching every man with all wisdom,
that we may present every man complete in
Christ. And for this purpose also I labor,
striving according to His power, which mightily
works within me" (Colossians 1:28-29).

By thinking specifically about each level and what God is doing in believers at those various stages, we then can better know how to work alongside our Lord.

The main reason for the lack of discipleship in our churches around the world seems to be the willingness to disengage from Jesus' command. Our solution will be to affirm God's life that He has given to His people, depend on God's desire to develop that life, encourage His people to grow in those specific ways, and foster a spirit among them to discover how God wants them to do the same with others.

An urgent need to prioritize

Significant positive changes will only come when we constrain ourselves and our institutions to prioritize this spiritual life process in our training. Integration of these key insights into our time with students and people is critical.

If God's people are not growing, then we as trainers are failing. A plant continues to grow, gain in size and maturity with the goal of producing fruit and multiplying itself. If a plant stops growing, the attentive farmer knows that this is nearly always a negative sign of disease or lack of water and nutrition, which could lead eventually to death.

The church faces a huge problem from not enabling God's people to grow. Lukewarmness is commonplace. The problem is compounded by Christian training schools, seminaries, and churches not properly producing godly leaders that know how to equip their students in godly living and intimacy with God.

Stepping into a greater faith

Without the belief that God can change others to grow to their fullness, then there will be no godly training. The church will default to a pretense of godliness and religiosity which kills rather than focuses on the author of life and the real life development that can and should occur in all believers.

When we again affirm what God is doing in us through the spiritual life process by the power of the Holy Spirit, then we will see the life of God once again thrive in our midst. This is the life core, the DNA of the church. May we stand as God's workman and foster the churches' growth into the fullest stage where it bears the light and love of God–this our ultimate goal.

"...Blessed be His glorious name forever; and may the whole earth be filled with His glory. Amen, and Amen" (Psalm 72:19).

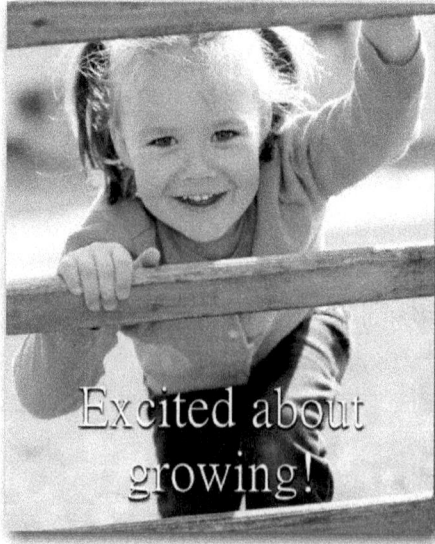

Excited about growing!

Lessons

- Although the spiritual life process is hidden from sight, its truth and developmental path is made known by God and hinted at in physical growth.

- All of God's people have a serious obligation to nurture the growth of their own spiritual life as well as others around them.

- As leaders in God's church, we must abide by the urgency of Christ's command and shift our priorities and activities to make sure God's people are spiritually growing and learning how to help others grow into godly men and women.

- God is very willing to work with us in this endeavor of nurturing spiritual life no matter how impossible it might seem. God's purpose is for His people to grow into His likeness and bear fruit and thus grandly accomplish His purposes on earth.

- God is most glorified when we, by His grace and company, become more like Him our Father, and accomplish His good works, "That they may see your good works, and glorify your Father who is in heaven" (Matthew 5:16).

Memorize & Meditate

Colossians 1:28-29

Assignment

➡ Start where you are. Commit yourself to focusing on releasing God's life force in your own life and in those around you.

➡ Acknowledge any areas of unbelief that has been seeded in your own heart. Repent from them. Here are some suggestions. Confess that, "I have doubts that...."

- ...God's people are able to grow to their fullest.

- ...God is actively working to accomplish His grand life purposes in my life or others.

- ...this life change is that important.

- ...I can change in one or more areas of my life.

- ...God's main purposes of training should center on nurturing the spiritual life."

➡ Rewrite Colossians 1:28-29 in your own words and personalize it, (i.e. Use 'I' and 'me').

➡ Make it your highest honor to bring God glory by working along with Him in helping His people grow and carry out His purposes.

➡ Pause and seek the Lord to see if He places any immediate steps in your mind that you need to take. If so, list them and put a time next to them when you will begin their implementation.

-

-

~ Appendices ~

#1-6

Appendix 1: Guide to Excellent Teaching

This diagram summarizes the two main principles behind *The Life Core*. The church rarely combines the insights of The Life Analogy along with The Growth Analogy and, as a result, the power and focus needed for a vibrant life and ministry has been lacking.

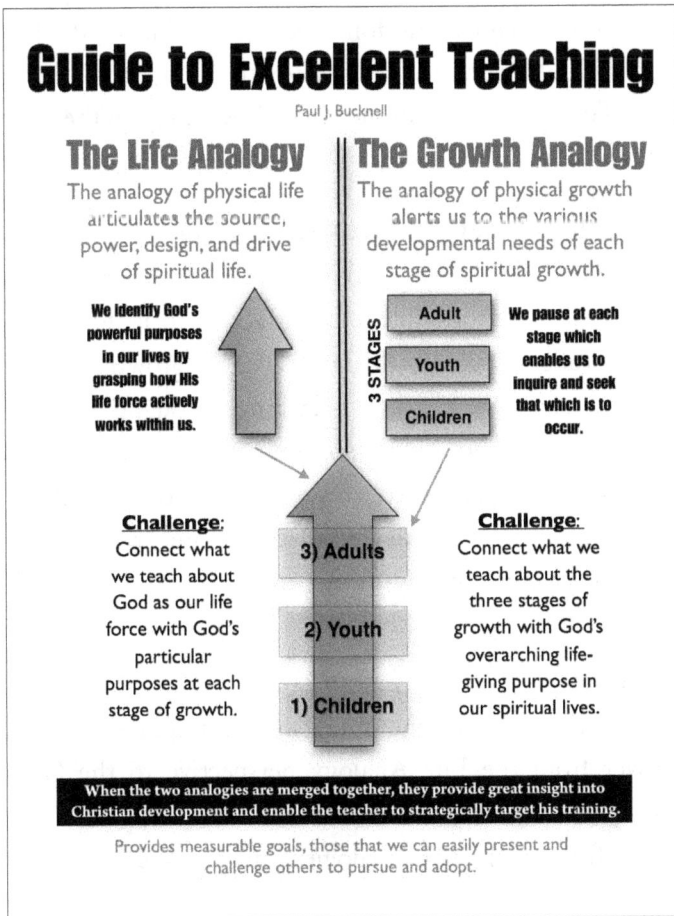

Guide to Excellent Teaching

Paul J. Bucknell

The Life Analogy

The analogy of physical life articulates the source, power, design, and drive of spiritual life.

We identify God's powerful purposes in our lives by grasping how His life force actively works within us.

Challenge:
Connect what we teach about God as our life force with God's particular purposes at each stage of growth.

The Growth Analogy

The analogy of physical growth alerts us to the various developmental needs of each stage of spiritual growth.

We pause at each stage which enables us to inquire and seek that which is to occur.

Challenge:
Connect what we teach about the three stages of growth with God's overarching life-giving purpose in our spiritual lives.

3 STAGES

Adult

Youth

Children

3) Adults

2) Youth

1) Children

When the two analogies are merged together, they provide great insight into Christian development and enable the teacher to strategically target his training.

Provides measurable goals, those that we can easily present and challenge others to pursue and adopt.

When merging these two analogies together, their synergetic power comes to life. Together they reveal the power of effective training and present insights, bringing much-needed encouragement into our personal lives and ministries.

The Challenge for the Life Analogy

The Christian's life-power, sourced by the Holy Spirit, enriches our spiritual lives and produces substantial growth. Most believers have never, however, considered how Christian development takes place in stages. This oversight has resulted in a shotgun approach, hoping some good will come out of it. Without the insights from the Growth Analogy, thoughts like, "I know I should grow but don't know how" can cast doubts on God's faithfulness and power. Growth is expected, but the means of growth, as seen in the Growth Analogy on the right, is missing.

The Challenge for the Growth Analogy

Many other believers, not conscious of God's presence and power in them, perform like religious actors. Teaching plans are enacted, students take notes, but power for growth, as seen in the Life Analogy on the left, is lacking. Thoughts like, "I am pursuing growth but don't see myself growing" can cause weariness and despair of ever overcoming unto the fullness of Christ. The spiritual life devoid of power and overall purpose must come to grasp the means of growth and be united with its life power (from the Life Analogy).

Summary

Excellent teaching on the spiritual life requires a constant crossover from the Life Analogy perspective to the Growth Analogy framework and vice-a-versa. Only by combining these insights from these two analogies can we keep focused on Christ-filled living.

➡ For larger pdf version: www.foundationsforfreedom.net/dl/d1-libr/Life-Core/Excellent-teaching.pdf

Appendix 2: The Analogies of Life

God's physical world can greatly deepen our understanding of spiritual truths. God makes the most important spiritual truths amazingly clear when we study the analogies He gives for life. Here are four life analogies. Start from the bottom like a plant.

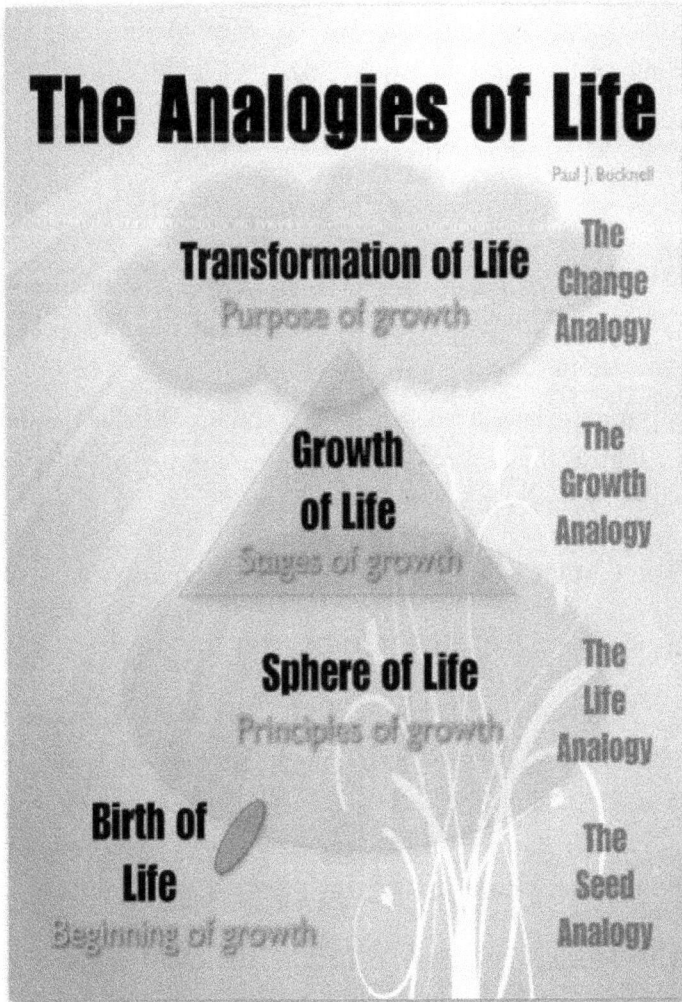

The Analogies of Life

Paul J. Bucknell

Transformation of Life
Purpose of growth
The Change Analogy

Growth of Life
Stages of growth
The Growth Analogy

Sphere of Life
Principles of growth
The Life Analogy

Birth of Life
Beginning of growth
The Seed Analogy

1. The Birth of Life – The seed analogy

Beginning of spiritual growth

"Truly, truly, I say to you, unless a grain of wheat falls into the earth and dies, it remains by itself alone; but if it dies, it bears much fruit. He who loves his life loses it; and he who hates his life in this world shall keep it to life eternal" (John 12:24-25).

"For you have been born again not of seed which is perishable but imperishable, that is, through the living and abiding word of God" (1 Peter 1:23).

2. The Sphere of Life – The life analogy

Principles of spiritual growth

"He who believes in the Son has eternal life; but he who does not obey the Son shall not see life, but the wrath of God abides on him" (John 3:36).

"But these have been written that you may believe that Jesus is the Christ, the Son of God; and that believing you may have life in His name" (John 20:31).

3. The Growth of Life – The growth analogy

Stages of spiritual growth

"I have written to you, children, because you know the Father. I have written to you, fathers, because you know Him who has been from the beginning. I have written to you, young men, because you are strong, and the word of God abides in you, and you have overcome the evil one" (1 John 2:13-14).

4. The Transformation of Life – The change analogy

Purpose of spiritual growth

"38 But God gives it a body just as He wished, and to each of the seeds a body of its own. All flesh is not the same flesh, but there is one flesh of men, and another flesh of beasts, and another flesh of birds, and another of fish.

40 There are also heavenly bodies and earthly bodies, but the glory of the heavenly is one, and the glory of the earthly is another... So also is the resurrection of the dead. It is sown a perishable body, it is raised an imperishable body" (1 Corinthians 15:38-42).

➡ For larger pdf version: www.foundationsforfreedom.net/dl/d1-libr/Life-Core/Analogies_Life.pdf

Appendix 3: The Flow

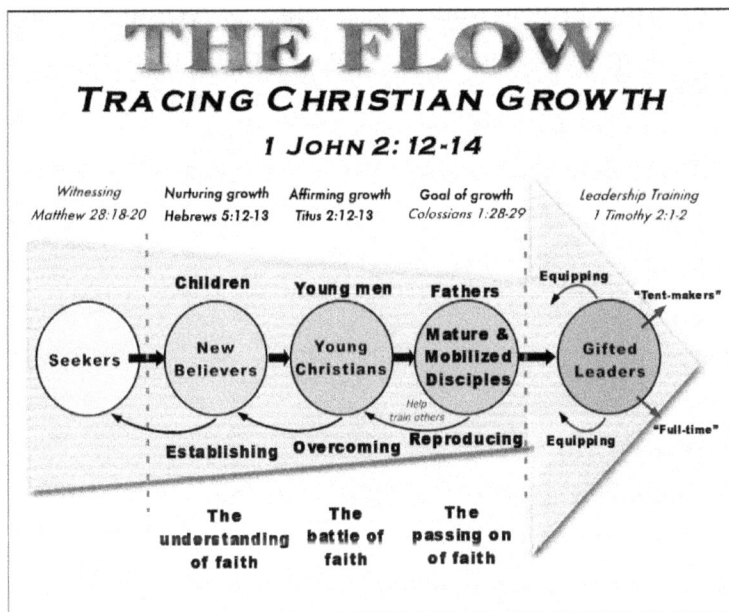

THE FLOW
TRACING CHRISTIAN GROWTH
1 JOHN 2: 12-14

Witnessing	*Nurturing growth*	*Affirming growth*	*Goal of growth*	*Leadership Training*
Matthew 28:18-20	*Hebrews 5:12-13*	*Titus 2:12-13*	*Colossians 1:28-29*	*1 Timothy 2:1-2*

Children   Young men   Fathers   Equipping

Seekers → New Believers → Young Christians → Mature & Mobilized Disciples → Gifted Leaders   "Tent-makers"

Help train others

Establishing   Overcoming   **Reproducing**   Equipping   "Full-time"

The understanding of faith   The battle of faith   The passing on of faith

By Paul J. Bucknell and Hugo Cheng

The above diagram of *The Flow* from 1 John 2:12-14 captures both the (1) powerful purpose of God by the motion of a wave along with (2) the ways of God, seen in what happens at each of the three stages of spiritual development.

The dotted lines are not technically part of the picture seen in 1 John, but we add the two sections in, at the beginning and the end, to give a more complete picture of the church. The seeker stage is where God is prodding people to come to know Him. The end point on the diagram serves as an amplification of a subset of the third stage which greatly shapes the direction of the church. These equippers, full-time or not, reinvest their energies into building up the people of God.

The divine life-giving river continually flows into His people to create godly character at every stage and is best seen as their growing faith. The more they know God through faith, the closer to God they live and better are able to carry out His grand purposes. All glory to God who initiated and will perpetuate His holy work. The existence of such truth should wake us up to respond to our Lord's mighty work in this world so that it might powerful touch our lives and training.

➡ For larger pdf version.

Appendix 4: Integration at Its Best

By Paul J. Bucknell and Kin Wee Choo

For organizations and institutions to be used of the Lord, the individuals, leaders, members, and coworkers, must remain close to Him.

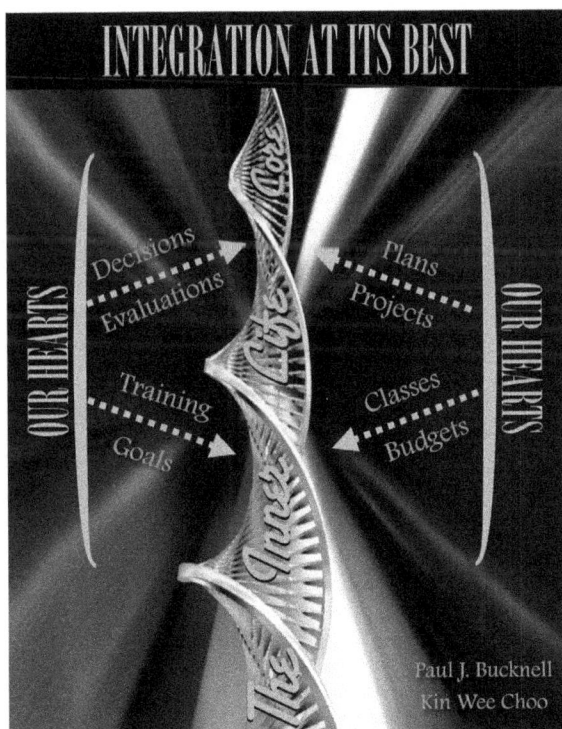

The chart's central spiral represents the primary way God's Spirit seeks to influence our lives positively. God's purposes and the life-giving source remains central, but it only helps us when we constantly make ourselves along with the principles and values attentive to His purposes. As we seek Him, we entertain how He desires to work through our decisions, goals, lives, etc. The institution only remains helpful in its goals when those sensitive to the Spirit conduct evaluations, projects, classes, etc., in light of the Holy Spirit's powerful inner working.

Appendix 5: More on the Author

Paul has worked as an overseas church planter during the 1980s and pastored in America during the 1990s. God called him to establish *Biblical Foundations for Freedom* in 2000 and since then he has been actively writing, holding international Christian leadership training seminars and serving in the local church.

Paul's wide range of materials on Christian life, discipleship, godly living, leadership training, marriage, parenting, anxiety, Old and New Testament and other spiritual life topics provide special insights that are blended into his many books and media-rich training resources.

Paul has been married for more than thirty-five wonderful years. With eight children and five grandchildren, Paul and his wife Linda continually see God's blessings unfold in their lives.

➡ For more on Paul and Linda and the BFF ministry, check online.

Appendix 6: About *The Life Core*

Discover the path to the restoration of the church's vitality!

The Life Core identifies underlying causes to numerous shortcomings and stagnation plaguing the Christian church and proposes practical solutions on how to integrate God's life into the heart of the church through proper leadership training.

Effective training begins when a vision of the Lord, His work, and the church is passed on in such a way that God's people are invigorated by the Spirit to carry out His will.

God's people need to insist that their churches, seminaries, schools, and leaders present the power of God's truth in ways that transform, empower, and equip them to lead others to life transformation. Only then will the power of God's Word be released!